The Catholic Experience
of Small Christian Communities

The Catholic Experience of Small Christian Communities

Bernard J. Lee, S.M.

with
William V. D'Antonio

and
Virgilio Elizondo, Patricia O'Connell Killen,
Jeanette Rodriguez, Evelyn Eaton Whitehead,
James D. Whitehead

PAULIST PRESS
New York/Mahwah, N.J.

Cover design by Morris Berman Studio. Photo of St. Patrick's Church, Memphis, courtesy of the Paulist Development Office. Photo of small Christian community, courtesy of Bernard J. Lee, S.M.

Book design by Theresa M. Sparacio

Library of Congress Cataloging-in-Publication Data

Lee, Bernard J., 1932-
    The Catholic experience of small Christian communities / Bernard J. Lee with William V. D'Antonio and Virgilio Elizondo...[et al.].
        p.   cm.
    Includes bibliographical references.
    ISBN 0-8091-3937-5 (alk. paper)
    1. Christian communities—Catholic Church. 2. Basic Christian communities.
I. D'Antonio, William V. II. Elizondo, Virgilio P. III. Title.
BX2347.7.L44 2000
262'.26—dc21

                                                              00-021007

Published by Paulist Press
997 Macarthur Boulevard
Mahwah, New Jersey 07430

www.paulistpress.com

Printed and bound in the
United States of America

Contents

Centers of Meaning

Just getting through life involves having to figure a lot of things out.

A lot of people are looking for help in figuring out what to do, in figuring out what is really going on in a situation, and in figuring out what our whole situation actually means.

The help most people really want is a community of people in whose company they can do their own "figuring"—honestly, truthfully, and with a sense of integrity.

What a gift it is if we are able to find a home place, a community of people who have really figured out how to go about figuring things out and thus live genuine lives!

Developing that capacity more strongly is some of the most important work the Christian churches in our society have to do—now.

Craig Dykstra
Initiatives in Religion
Winter 1998, 1–2, *passim*

Preface:
Whose Book Is This?

While I accept responsibility for the final shape of this report in book form, I want to say that, except for whatever aberrations and eccentricities I am responsible, it is *our* book. The shape of the research has been a co-creation of the two teams, the theologians and the researchers. The basic shape of the book is also the outcome of extended conversation together. Further, members of the theological team have taken responsibility for presenting and interpreting different parts of the research. I have had at hand hard copy and disks from the team and have used them throughout. All that I have written is nourished by remarkable conversations with the theological team, and between the theological team and the research team. We have met several times together for days at a time, and more often in telephone conferences.

Collaboration with a hard-nosed and dialogic sociologist like William D'Antonio has been a larger gift to this project than any reflections could convey. As the piles of tables and data stacked higher and higher on the desk, we theologians sensed quickly that, being without a sociologist's *nose*, we needed interpretive assistance. Dr. D'Antonio has, with consummate patience, attached commentaries on the data to the many tables, which greatly facilitated theological reflection.

Dr. D'Antonio has been a meticulous editorial conversation partner in the shaping of each chapter. He has prepared all of the materials that appear in the important appendices.

It has been, and continues to be, a pleasure to get some reliable glimpses of a significant, moving adventure in the U.S. Catholic Church, and to do so in the company of extraordinary colleagues.

1

Snapshots of a Church in Motion
The Existence and Growth of SCCs

Small Christian Communities Matter

Karl Rahner, whose theological and pastoral judgments were equally acute, wrote the following words over a quarter century ago:

> The basic communities…will have to develop for the most part out of existing parishes…. This does not exclude the fact that a basic community has its own pronounced character, gives itself a certain structure and (if you like to use the term) constitution, and that it really demands from its freely associated members something which goes completely beyond what a parishioner today has to do for the ordinary parish…. The church of the future will be one built from below by basic communities as a result of free initiative and association. We should make every effort not to hold up this development, but to promote it and direct it on to the right lines…. The church will exist only by being constantly renewed by a free decision of faith…in the midst of a secular world…for the church cannot be a real factor in secular history except as sustained by the faith on the part of human beings…. Basic communities will in fact emerge from below, even though it will be a call from the gospel and the message of the church coming out of the past… (Rahner, 1974, 108–15, *passim*).

While small Christian communities (SCCs) are not, in any simple way, the future of the Catholic Church, there is probably no future that will not find itself shaped by their worldwide emergence.

That new church will almost surely have a place for them because they will have made a place for themselves. They seem, in fact, to be doing that.

There are many themes in Rahner's remarks that our research suggests have proved accurate. SCCs will, by and large, come out of parish life, but will come forth to meet needs and interests beyond what parish life ordinarily meets. They will develop their own character, and the church will be challenged to address what emerges— a source of *the new* from below. The new will have been called forth by the gospel and by the ancient experience of the church.

The free initiative and voluntary association that energize these small Christian communities are indeed consistent with the people of God ecclesiology of Vatican II. The baptized are assuming responsibility. SCCs will prove to be—indeed, are proving to be—a dynamic that will give the church a will and an effective voice in secular history. These themes, sounded by Rahner's remarks, will recur throughout the book, especially in chapter five.

The story is told that one day after philosophy class was over, a student walked up to his Harvard professor, the renowned philosopher Alfred North Whitehead, and inquired: "Dr. Whitehead, how would you characterize reality?" Whitehead put down the books he was carrying, remained silent for a long time, then said: "It matters. It has consequences." He then picked his books up and exited. That, I would say, is the collective judgment of those of us who have worked on this research project: Small Christian communities matter; they have consequences. Having consequences is how anything matters.

At Once Ancient and New

Something important is happening in the Catholic Church around the world. There's no master plan for it that anyone has contrived, unless perhaps the Holy Spirit has done it. And that's an interpretation to which this study is quite open.

This book is a report upon a systematic effort to describe and interpret this "new thing," or this "new old thing." The research, conducted between 1995 and 1998, was funded by a generous grant from Lilly Endowment, Inc., to the Institute for Ministry at Loyola University. For the thousands of members of small Christian communities, for many of us interested in understanding what is happening in the church in which these communities are emerging, in the name of the theologians and researchers that have carried out the study, especially in the name of Dr. William D'Antonio, principal researcher, and in my own behalf as project director, I offer an expression of profound gratitude to Lilly Endowment, and especially to Sr. Jeanne Knoerle, S.P., religion program director, for her lively interest and support. As a member of the religious branch of the Marianist Family, for whom communities-in-permanent-mission are a fundamental life form, I welcome the good news that this study is able to affirm.

The good news is that Christians are gathering on their own initiative to form communities—usually small ones that are often supported by priests and religious sisters and brothers. But the membership and the leadership are largely lay. The people of God are doing this, and what they are doing looks a lot like the form of church that was the only form in the early centuries. But it is not simply a repetition or a retrieval.

Imagine it this way. The setting is a home, with about a dozen adults and some children. It's informal. What else can you be with young ones ranging from eight months to age 16? Someone has been telling the story of Jesus, and others are telling their own stories, sometimes personal, sometimes from the town in which they live or from the places where they work—their social stories. They encourage these stories to connect: Word and world. Livable meaning is being generated, and that's the major *magic*. They are centers of meaning for Catholics seeking to live their faith—to live their lives—meaningfully.

These communities often move from Liturgy of the Word to table fellowship, sometimes with a sharing of bread and cup, not a Eucharist, but a table experience that remembers that Catholic culture is eucharistic, inside of Mass or out. Or it may be agape and potluck. (There is one group of contemporary small Christian communities that does gather regularly for Eucharist; most SCC members, however, participate in their parishes.)

This could have been a description of a group of Christians in northern Palestine or southern Syria in the year 80, in a home that belonged to a follower of Jesus named Matthew. The community told the story of Jesus each time it came together, a story that gathered power, structure, definition, and developed into the Gospel of Matthew.

Or this could be a description of something happening in a home in Seattle, or St. Louis, or New Orleans, or Coral Gables, or Richmond, or Washington, D.C., or Bangor, Maine. Today, too, like the story of old, the good news is gathering people in small groups, often in homes. These gatherings are building structures in which Christians are giving themselves definition. SCCs are perhaps maturing into still another new story, one called "contemporary Catholic life."

SCCs are places where Catholics make Catholic meaning *together* from which they choose to live their lives. *Together* is important. The web of committed relationships is a constitutive dynamic in the meaning-making process. They are doing their best to figure things out together. "We have changed the way we think. Now it comes out of the Gospel. It's that in reflecting on the Word, and bringing it to life, we analyze ourselves. Then we are capable of responding to the project of Jesus." People gather together in community to tell their stories, bring their experience into dialogue with their faith, and leave with some sense of meaning. Not just "head" meaning. Meaning for living, "the project of Jesus." Knowing what difference it makes. Orienting a life. Shaping a social situation. That is a recurring theme in small Christian communities in the U.S. Catholic Church. "You stand back and say, 'wait, there may be another way of doing this…the work with small communities is underneath creating other styles of church.'" We need each other to make meaning out of our faith. "We talk about our real lives. We read the scriptures as a starting point, but it is not constructed by religious facts. The majority of people are hungry for that sort of approach to religion, if you will." That dynamic surfaces over and over in our research.

Like the Early Church

Members of these SCCs often understand this new experience as a retrieval of the major form for ecclesial gathering. The small Christian community or house church was, in fact, the normative basic unit of church life until Constantine and Theodosius gave Christianity the status of state religion in the mid-fourth century. "Yes, I think we are a way of being church…but a new way that's very ancient in our tradition…. That's what's been exciting for me to discern, that Paul wrote those letters to small house churches." The ancient roots, of course, are there, but this is not a mere retrieval. People in those early centuries built church upon a social form that is no longer part of our culture: the household. We sometimes use the expression household today, but it does not mean what it did in the early centuries of Mediterranean Graeco-Roman life. While this unit has something in common with extended family, it was a more formally recognized form of social life in the early centuries of the common era and included many who were not blood-kin (for example, business clients and other kinds of professional connections). In those centuries the small Christian community was a natural response to natural social structures.

But Also a New Church

Today's small Christian communities are an increasingly significant response to the good news of Jesus Christ all around the world, but are shaped by other social realities than were those early communities. In other countries and on other continents there are other names: base communities *(communidades de base)*, basic ecclesial communities, basic Christian communities, and so forth. Their reasons for being formed and their shapes vary from country to country and continent to continent.

The base communities of Latin America arose out of catechumenal efforts in Brazil in the late 1950s. Instruction was broadcast on the radio to mountain areas without resident pastors. Catechists would come every month or two and meet with those who listened to the radio broadcasts. Sometimes village facilitators would meet more regularly. Communities formed from the gathering of Christians seeking to deepen their faith—a dynamic not unlike people who gathered for renewal under the RENEW program, and found that their gatherings were bonding them into communities of faith. Such communities multiplied quickly in Latin America, taking on many configurations from country to country, with an increasing interest in the liberative power of Christian faith.

In this book, however, we are tracking a development in the U.S. Catholic Church, one that goes by many names: small Christian communities, small church communities, house churches, communities of faith, faith sharing groups, and so forth. In this report, for convenience, we choose to use the designation *small Christian community* because that is probably the most widely used expression in U.S. Catholicism. Some of the small groups and communities use other designations. And there is some movement afoot to speak of *small church communities*, as a reminder that the active dynamics of churchhood are constitutive.

The configuration of these small communities often differs significantly from one region to another because sociocultural location has so much impact upon the shape of human community. Responding to individualism in U.S. culture is one contextualizing feature of the communities included in this study.

In the 1830s an astute visitor to the United States from France, Alexis de Tocqueville, described in vivid detail the individualism that he felt characterized U.S. culture.

> Individualism is a calm and considered feeling which disposes each citizen to isolate himself from the mass of his fellows and withdraw into the circle of family and friends; with this little society formed to his taste, he gladly leaves the greater society to look after itself (de Tocqueville, 1969, 506).

In the last 40 years, successive sociological studies on our American world note a kind of cultural loneliness that has emerged: *The Lonely Crowd: A Study of the Changing American Character*, David Riesman, et al; *The Fall of Public Man*, Richard Sennett; *The Pursuit of Loneliness: American Culture at the Breaking Point*, Philip Slater. The best-known recent study is detailed in *Habits of the Heart*. Robert Bellah and his co-researchers note that simultaneously there is a hunger for community and a reluctance to make the commitments necessary for community.

Perhaps the hunger for community is outstripping the resistances, for Robert Wuthnow notes in his Lilly-funded study that four out of every ten Americans belong to some kind of small group

(Wuthnow, 1994, 4). Most of these are support groups. It is certainly not a new phenomenon for Americans to belong to voluntary associations. What may be somewhat novel is the emergence of small Christian communities as a particular form of voluntary association. The appetite for group membership is a likely cultural factor in the emergence of SCCs in the U.S. Catholic Church.

Our research tells us, in fact, that the experience of community and relationships is one of the most satisfying aspects of SCC membership. The need for community is linked with strong spiritual hungers, and the SCC brings them together. "It's one thing to hear the Word of God," comments a community member, "but to be able to talk about it, and share about it, and how it applies to your daily life among your peers. It's so different [than Mass]. It's more life-giving, more enriching."

Why This Study?

Many of our interests as theologians, sociologists, and anthropologists coincide with concerns of the Religion Division of Lilly Endowment, Inc. We are interested in the actual practices of Christians for whom faith is a serious commitment. Small Christian communities are one of the places in Catholic life where committed people practice their faith. These are not the only places, of course, but they are the object of our study.

At a time when Catholics have increasingly absented themselves from regular church attendance, it is important to assess what makes some people do not less but more. And those who belong to small Christian communities are people who opt to do significantly more than parish life normally asks. Most of them give two or three hours additional time every week or two. The relational connections between members often get time and attention in addition to the regular gatherings. We want to know who these people are, what their practices are, why they engage in them, and what difference it makes.

Perhaps the main reason for this study of small Christian communities is the fact that *they exist* in sufficient numbers to have a presence and to invite interpretation. We are interested in why they were created in the first place and why people join and remain in them. It is almost too commonplace to say that the church is in a time of transition with all the disorientation that accompanies such transformation. I have indicated already the perception that SCCs are attractive because they are centers where people of faith can work at finding meaning—figuring out *how* to figure things out. There is also some real possibility, indeed probability, that forms of church that will break into some new settled order on the other side of these massive ecclesial adjustments are being experimented with, played with, in the serious life of small Christian communities (and elsewhere too, of course).

In chapter five, I will be suggesting that the category of *margins* helps interpret some aspects of SCC life, for in every healthy society there is some marginal activity where new things are being tried out—new ways of making meaning. I will offer theological reflection on the U.S. experience of small Christian communities (nourished by extensive conversation between members of the theological team). Our research also leads us to offer some pastoral recommendations.

Small Christian Communities in the U.S. Catholic Church

Based upon a large national survey and extensive regional sampling, we feel secure in our estimate of the existence, minimally, of 37,000 small Christian communities in the continental United States, with a membership of over a million (including adults and children). We say minimally, because we know of that number from our research; but we also know that our net has not caught all of them. A large majority (about 75 percent) of these communities have some kind of parish connection. This is a significant minority in a church of over 60 million, of whom only about a third are regularly participants in Sunday Eucharist. We know, then, that about one-in-twenty regular church-attending Catholics belongs to some kind of small Christian community— communities that are amazing in their variety, but share significant *soul*.

While these SCC Catholics resemble the general Catholic population on such issues as juggling competing claims between traditional church teaching and conclusions to which their own experience leads them, SCC members are more likely to give the tradition a serious hearing. The church allegiance of SCC Catholics is significantly stronger than that of Catholics who are not members of SCCs. Except for Hispanic/Latino communities, SCC Catholics are better educated and more affluent than the average U.S. Catholic where, in fact, education and fiscal status are higher than the general population.

Although they constitute a small percentage of total SCCs, members of two groups that will be distinguished shortly (Call to Action communities, and Eucharist Centered Communities) are markedly committed to social agenda. Their members are the best educated of SCCs and the most critical of church and culture. By critical I mean a readiness, even an inclination, to assess both strengths and weaknesses.

Snapshots of a Moving Picture

This book reports on research that catches small Christian communities in the U.S. Catholic Church at specific moments in their development, not all at an identical moment in time. While most of our *snapshots* are from a narrower time slot, some of our data cover a larger period. Our research, however, is not longitudinal, that is, we have not tracked with the same communities or the same community members over time.

In the brief historical reflection that follows, I hope to indicate clearly that we are catching something important that came from somewhere and is going somewhere. But what we have are still shots of great motion. But the still shot is finely enough grained to let us decipher and guess at its character and its possible directions.

My reason for detailing a dozen or so years of SCC development in the following paragraphs is basically to substantiate the judgment that a lot has happened, is still happening, and will probably continue to happen (since there are no indicators of a slow-down). Here, then, is a sketch of the motion.

It was not until the early 1980s that small Christian communities began to have a face in the U.S. Catholic Church. Small group life is a phenomenon in many Protestant traditions as well, and frequently so in evangelical traditions. The Catholic expression, however, is the object of our research and theological interpretation.

There are precedents in the U.S. Catholic experience which, while not exactly SCC in character, familiarized a part of Catholic culture with small groups gathered for faith reasons: sodalities, Catholic Action, Christian Family Movement, Legion of Mary, Cursillo, Marriage Encounter, and so forth.

In the years following Vatican II, a different kind of small group began gathering, akin in some respects to SCCs. They were sometimes identified as *underground churches.* These were often people in search of more participative liturgical experience, and they were also people with social commitment. A publication of experimental eucharistic prayers was even published during this time entitled *Underground Mass Book.* Some of the longer-lived SCCs our research encounters have roots in the underground church.

In the early 1980s a bi-monthly publication, *Gathering*, was initiated by Sheed & Ward (owned by the *National Catholic Reporter*), to serve the needs of these new small communities. When Michael Cowan and I were working on the manuscript for *Dangerous Memories* between1984 and 1986 we had to depend upon oral reports from SCCs we'd heard of or knew about, including our own. Not much was visible, so we frequently made educated, intuitional guesses.

In the subsequent years much has transpired, including the creation of Buena Vista, a national network of SCCs. Buena Vista has a quarterly periodical, in-house publications, and holds an annual convention. RENEW was already a popular approach to updating and spiritual renewal in Catholic parishes, the brainchild of Msgr. Tom Kleissler and colleagues. People formed small groups and met in homes over a number of seasons. When the RENEW seasons of gatherings were completed, many groups chose to continue because the experience had been so rewarding. RENEW was not originally intended to spawn SCCs. However, our research tells us that RENEW has been a great primer of interest in them. RENEW itself now offers a full range of programs and resources to nurture SCCs in the post-RENEW life. RENEW, which began in the U.S. church, is used in other countries and has become

RENEW International—a gift, we believe, from the U.S. experience to churches in other lands.

A priest in the Detroit archdiocese, Fr. Art Baranowski, began a parish experiment in which SCCs were not just another program supported by a parish, but became part of a model for the restructuring of a parish into a community of communities. In the early centuries of church life, house churches were the basic units of ecclesial reality. These units built up into what later became parishes and dioceses. It takes a different imagination about church to see a parish *built up* out of small church communities rather than to think of a larger unit that is *broken down* into small church communities. Father Art and Carrie Piro have provided leadership in what has become the National Alliance for Parishes Restructuring into Communities. Each small community has a trained pastoral facilitator. Since much effective ministry takes place among members, the pastor of the parish becomes something of a pastor to pastors (i.e., the pastoral facilitators). While no parish has succeeded in bringing all members into SCCs, enough sometimes join to affect the texture of parish life. SCCs are a nurturing place for new parish leadership. Perhaps the major contribution of the Baranowski model is that it has introduced an alternative vision, a re-imagination, of what a parish can be. It makes us rethink the structures we have taken for granted. Social imagination has to be one of the most prized graces to a church in the midst of such fundamental upheaval.

The publications that have emerged to serve SCCs are also a measure of movement and development. The Pastoral Office for Small Christian Communities in Hartford, Connecticut, directed by Bro. Bob Moriarty, S.M., began operation in 1986. The office prepares a lectionary-based booklet called *Quest* to guide parish SCCs in their celebration of the Word in Hartford. SCCs in many other places began to use *Quest*. Currently, there are four editions of *Quest* each year. In the spring of 1992, 11,300 copies of *Quest* were printed (each printing); in spring 1997 the number was about 20,000.

Sunday by Sunday, edited by Joan Mitchell, a Sister of St. Joseph, located in the Minneapolis/St. Paul area, is an evolution of a project begun in 1988, which was directed to the high-school level. Market research revealed there was little to expect in the way of a parish market. But the risk was taken to produce materials for that market anyway. Although it took some years to break open, parish has come to be the market mainstay. *Sunday by Sunday* is a lectionary-based scripture guide prepared for adult SCCs. The publication *Spirit* is a lectionary-based guide for teen groups. The format for both is very engaging. Between 1991 and 1992 there were 11,300 subscriptions to *Sunday by Sunday*. In 1996 the subscription base was about 20,000. At this writing, the number of subscriptions for 1997 is 3,000 ahead of 1996. Once again, that's a measure of motion.

Exploring the Sunday Readings is published by Twenty-Third Publications. It grew out of a smaller publication, *Gathering Place*, a quarterly for SCCs. Although it did not find a large audience, there was significant interest in its attention to scripture. The monthly publication of *Exploring*, a lectionary-based guide to scripture for use in groups, began in 1990. By 1994, circulation was at 72,000. Circulation in 1998 was 100,000. While intended for use in small Christian communities, some parishes insert it into the bulletin (there are 20 subscriptions with orders for over a thousand).

At Home with the Word, published by Liturgy Training Publications, first appeared in 1984. In 1987, LTP printed 50,000 copies, in 1992, 132,500 copies, in 1997, 146,740 copies, and in 1998, 175,000. The lectionary-based text takes into consideration both the Roman Catholic Lectionary and the Revised Common Lectionary. Martin Connell, LTP editor, says that there seems to be a large appeal to more rural areas (less to the big cities on the east or west coasts), and that the clientele is largely but not exclusively Catholic.

It is not possible to make an exact correlation between the increase in publications and the increase in SCCs, in part because parishes also use some of these materials for general parish distribution. But it would be foolhardy not to see the increase in SCCs mirrored in the dramatic increase in the materials prepared specifically for their use. These materials are also important because they provide assistance in the interpretation of the scriptures, and that helps avoid some of the fundamentalistic leanings that sometimes develop out of a hunger for clear, unassailable meaning.

In this present decade there have been two international theological consultations on SCCs in the United States, bringing together members and representatives from all five continents. These were hosted by the University of Notre Dame and orchestrated by Rev. Robert Pelton, C.S.C.

During the dozen or so years upon which I am musing, the National Forum for Small Christian Communities was formed, networking diocesan personnel with responsibilities for helping to initiate and nurture SCCs. There has been collaboration between this forum and the North American Forum on the Catechumenate, with common interest in the development of SCCs as catechumenal communities to which catechumens are "apprenticed" (in place of RCIA teams that are formed each year for new catechumens).

There have now been two national congresses of SCCs, coordinated by three networks, Buena Vista, the National Alliance for Parishes Restructuring into Communities, and the National Forum for Small Christian Communities. The first was held at St. Thomas University in St. Paul in 1993, the second at Loyola and Tulane universities in New Orleans in 1997.

Currently, there is a national association, The Associates, under the direction of Jean Sonnenberg, serving religious orders that are developing lay associate membership. A quarterly publication fosters communication and dialogue. Sisters Louise Hembrecht and Paula Rae Rose conducted a survey of 381 women's religious communities, of which 279 (72.23 percent) responded (completed in 1995). Of the communities responding, 80 percent presently have an associate program (some 14,500 associate members). Sonnenberg indicates that a large number of these have all or many of the characteristics of SCCs. We became aware of this study and this organization too late to incorporate associate communities of religious orders in our research.

It would perhaps take a book just to document the growth in SCC activity over the past dozen or so years, a growth that has been formidable.

There is no reason to think that the movement has reached its zenith. We are in motion, somewhere on new journeys into ecclesiality, *viatores*, as Thomas Aquinas called us, people of the road. It is because we are on the road and still going that research like ours and a book like this about the research findings are but snapshots of motion, arguably of significant motion. At least that is the perspective put forward here.

Purview of What Follows

In the second chapter, I will describe the research instruments that were developed for this project and indicate the way we have grouped SCCs in this study. For those who want a fuller, technical description of the research and its methodology, Dr. William D'Antonio, the principal researcher for this project, has offered a detailed narrative in Appendix II.

In the third chapter, I will characterize the members of small Christian communities and indicate the reasons they offer for joining.

Chapter four will survey the major regular activities of SCCs, situating them within both Catholic and U.S. cultures. We are interested in continuities (how people benefit from the wisdom of the tradition) and discontinuities (new forms of church-hood, new modes and places of gathering). "What difference it makes" is the focus of the latter part of chapter four. We want to hear whether the satisfaction experienced in being a member of an SCC is the same as the reasons people gave for joining in the first place. We are also interested in what impact people perceive SCCs to have, not just on their own lives, but on the larger community, both ecclesial and civil.

In chapter five I will venture beyond the clear logic of the data to offer some theological interpretation on what we feel we have described, and, in some cases, to intimate what the experience for small Christian communities might be saying to and about the future of the U.S. Catholic Church.

There are two appendices. In the first, Dr. William D'Antonio sumarizes what we have learned about SCCs on college and university campuses. Since our data are less complete on these communities, I have not included them in the body of the book, but there is certainly enough to be able to draw some useful inferences.

Appendix II is a more detailed statement of the methodology for this study than the one I offer in chapter two. This appendix is offered for those with technical interest in how the research was conducted.

2

The Shape of the Research
Its Scope and Limitations

Introduction

This research project has had a long incubation period. I would like to share with readers how and why it emerged. Then, in the remainder of the chapter, I will describe the dynamic inner workings of the project. The model of practical theology elucidates the way in which mutuality between theological and social scientific inquiry and interpretation has shaped this project from start to finish.

The Genesis of the Research Project

Energized by good experiences of small community life in Berkeley, St. Louis, and Collegeville, Minnesota, in the early 1980s I submitted an article on small Christian communities to *Gathering*, a publication for SCCs that was part of the *National Catholic Reporter* operation. Bob Heyer, who was editor of both *Gathering* and Sheed & Ward Publishers, invited a book project on the topic. With my colleague Michael Cowan (a fellow member of the same SCC), we wrote *Dangerous Memories: House Churches and Our American Story*, published in 1986.

In the summer of 1989, supported by a grant from the St. Louis Province Marianists, Michael Cowan and I hosted a five-day meeting in the rustic Texas hill country near Kerrville to dialogue three voices: the SCC experience, the institutional Catholic Church, and U.S. culture. The fifteen or so participants were

18

people with the background and experience that enabled them to speak on behalf of each of these three areas. I recall, for example, the institutional voice saying of SCCs that "you could become elitist." SCCs said of themselves: "We are populist to the core." The U.S. experience said: "If you were a little more 'American,' you'd be more comfortable with pluralism in Catholic community." We left the meeting naming the need for public conversation to continue in some way or another, and sensing that the time might be ripe for a more systematic piece of research on a phenomenon that was becoming more visible.

A second Marianist grant, this time from the Cincinnati Province, supported a larger gathering than the previous one, with a possible research proposal as the major agenda item. Three kinds of people attended the 1992 gathering at Loyola University, New Orleans: those with specific connections to SCC networks, such as Buena Vista, Parishes Restructuring into Small Communities, the NCCB Office for Hispanic Affairs, and the Mexican American Cultural Center; theologians interested in trying to interpret this phenomenon ecclesiologically; and those with research interests, among them Fr. Joseph Fichter (a short time before his death) and William V. D'Antonio, who would become the principal researcher for our study. We concluded that it would be very useful research, and also recognized that it would be a complex task to locate the communities and to structure research instruments. How sociological and anthropological would our research interests be? How theological would they be? And how would these intersect and complement?

Dr. D'Antonio and I continued discussion after the meeting and drew up a proposal that went through multiple drafts. In 1995, with encouragement and support from Sr. Jeanne Knoerle, S.P., religion program director of Lilly Endowment, Inc., we submitted a planning grant proposal and were awarded the grant. This allowed us to conduct a large census of SCCs nationally to determine how a larger research project should be strategized. And then, in 1996, we received a generous grant from Lilly Endowment to conduct extensive and intensive research on "Small Christian Communities in the U.S. Catholic Church." How this grant was implemented and how the research has been conducted are the topics of this chapter for the general reader. (As I indicated earlier, Appendix II, prepared by Dr.

D'Antonio, offers a far more detailed description for the benefit of those with technical research interests.)

Practical Theology

Put simply, this research project is an important part of a community's conversation between its faith and its experience. In many ways, we, the theologians and researchers, are in the conversation as insiders as well as observers and interpreters. Generally, we are engaged from scholarly interests, from vested church interests, and for many of us, from deeply personal interests as small Christian community members. The work is conducted seriously and systematically so that ecclesial life can be nourished and transformed by the process. This is an exercise in practical theology, and some brief reflection upon its methods will elucidate the character of the study.

The term *practical theology* doesn't have one clear, univocal meaning, though there are two defined clusters of meanings. Both are valid and important, but significantly different. I want to indicate the sense of things within which we have operated.

One theological sensibility sees practical theology as the application of systematic theology to pastoral needs, or as specifically pastoral areas, such as homiletics or pastoral counseling. This is not the sense of practical theology that guides our research activities.

Another theological sensibility sees practical theology as a *form* rather than a *branch* of theology. David Tracy has described this form of theology as a mutually critical conversation between interpretations of faith and interpretations of the social worlds within which we live. I would add that practical theology also has strategic intentions: the transformation of ourselves and our world. *Conversion* is another word for it. We engage in theological reflection to make a difference. Practical theology is most authentically conducted within a community, by a community, for the sake of community. It involves a rhythm of action and reflection: reflection that nurtures action, and action that is the subject of further reflection. It is this latter sense that is largely at work in our research and our interpretation of the findings.

Theologians and researchers designed the research in phone conferencing, written correspondence, e-mail, faxes, and, above all, in significant face-to-face dialogue. Social scientists have guided the collection of data and provided social analysis into the phenomenon of small Christian communities. All of the theologians involved have written about and been concerned with theological method in their professional careers, and have contributed to both content and method in the research design. They have also helped frame the inquiry from the start.

The research design and its implementation have been under the astute direction of Dr. William D'Antonio. His long, highly successful career in the sociology of religion and, more specifically, his extensive research on the contemporary Catholic community have made available to this rather massive project an incredible savoir-faire.

In his analysis of biblical community, Paul Hanson speaks of a double exegesis: We are interpreting Word (which stands for all the resources of faith) and world (any and all of the contexts in which we live). These are the basic dynamics of both small Christian community life and practical theology. Gustavo Gutierrez has clearly seen the analogical connection between the life of small Christian communities and this particular model of theological activity:

> The course to be followed if one is to be a Christian is the basis for the direction in which one must move in order to do theology. It can be said, therefore, that our methodology is our spirituality (G. Gutierrez, 1990, 5).

Practical theology is a spiritually charged way of being Christian. I think it not inappropriate to see this project in that light as well as in the light of capable social scientific investigation and theological interpretation.

Theologian and Researcher Teams

Since this research bears the marks of those who planned it and carried it out, I would like to introduce the two teams (theologians and researchers). I have asked them to say something about their interests and backgrounds. These brief autobiographical statements are intended to display the interests and achievements that have nourished our study's double exegesis.

It has been my experience that true interdisciplinary conversation is quite difficult. I do not mean what happens when a person socialized profoundly in one discipline reads widely, and even deeply, in another. I am a theologian who has tried to become literate in the human sciences; I have a profound respect for empirical studies, but that is not my métier. By interdisciplinary, I mean a project whose outcome has been radically shaped by mutually interactive dialogue between persons whose basic instincts have been thoroughly socialized in different disciplines. In our case this comprises Catholic theology, comparative religions, history, social psychology, sociology, and anthropology. Numerically, theologians and sociologists are in the majority. I want to acknowledge from the outset that every part of this research was shaped by sustained conversation between committed members of these disciplines.

Professionally, this has been a remarkable experience. The researchers have often been asked by the theologians to gather information somewhat different in character from their usual wont, and the theologians have learned how to ask questions to gather desired information. Sometimes the theologians have learned that the amount of time and money it would take to gather certain kinds of information make certain of their proposed inquiries not possible. That's the professional side.

On the personal side, I must say the interaction has been exhilarating. The mutual respect and quality of animated and fascinated interaction exemplify healthy, respectful, straightforward conversation. We have learned from each other with appreciation and delight. I have asked members of these teams to introduce themselves. I think that from seeing each one's self characterization you will hear the amazing richness, breadth of interests, and well-practiced expertise that have been brought to bear on this research.

Dr. William V. D'Antonio, Catholic University of America. I am a sociologist with special interests in family, religion, ethnicity, and politics. A variety of issues, ideas, and theories crosscut these interests. Among those I am most concerned with at the present time are: the continuing struggle between personal autonomy and community, or the communitarian ethic; the growth and direction of small community; the impact of fertility trends on family and institutions; and the changing nature of authority within our social institutions, with particular attention to family, church, and government. I have been an active member of a small Eucharist centered community for some 14 years.

Dr. Virgilio Elizondo, Mexican American Cultural Center (MACC), San Antonio, Texas. As a Mexican-American raised in San Antonio, I have a strong interest in Mexican-American culture and how it and Catholic culture interact with and impact upon each other. And I am keenly interested in the pastoral implications. These interests were motivations for me in founding the Mexican American Cultural Center, and in functioning as its first president. Since that time I have been pastor of San Antonio's San Fernando Cathedral and have now returned as a faculty member to the MACC. My publications have addressed small Christian communities, the mestizo experience of Hispanic/Latinos, and the role of our Lady of Guadalupe in the faith of the Americas.

Dr. Dean Hoge, Catholic University of America. I am a sociologist of religion specializing in American church life. I am a Presbyterian layperson with a degree from an interdenominational divinity school. My past research has included studies of the Catholic priest shortage, Catholic evangelization, and the religion of Baby Boomer and post-Boomer Catholics. I have also done Protestant studies on denominational trends, financial giving, and Baby Boomers. Currently I am studying young adult Catholics and evaluating the effects of the RCIA.

Dr. Guillermina Jasso, University of New York. My work focuses on comparison processes, the human sense of justice, and international migration. To better understand them, I use mathematical and statistical methods for both theoretical and empirical analysis. My larger purpose is to identify the basic forces governing human behavior, to describe their operation, and to derive their implications. I have a special affection for the saints who have thought deeply about human nature: Augustine, Anselm, Ignatius of Loyola, and Teresa of Avila. Their writings provide illuminating inspiration, and, indeed, lead directly to my short list of current candidates for the basic forces governing human behavior: knowing the causes of things; judging the goodness of things; being perfect; and being free.

Dr. Patricia Killen, Pacific Lutheran University. I am an American church historian with a focus on the Roman Catholic

Church in the United States. I am particularly interested in describing the ways ordinary people have related to and drawn on their religious heritages in the shifting social and cultural contexts of the nineteenth and twentieth centuries and how they have, in the process, both been shaped by and have themselves transformed these heritages. This question has necessitated expanding my research and thinking into the fields of theological reflection, sociological studies of community, and ecclesiology. Working across the boundaries of disciplines to explore the relationship among communities, religious heritages, and social contexts has mirrored my own experience of moving between the worlds of a rural, ethnic Catholic subculture and the academy.

Dr. Bernard Lee, S.M., Loyola University New Orleans. I am a theologian with special interests in ecclesiology, Christology, and sacramental theology. I have also been associated with the empirical wing of process theology, which accounts for my sense of the importance of empirical interpretation to theological interpretation. My efforts to understand SCCs in the contemporary church have led me to some fascination with *margins* as both a sociological and hermeneutical category relevant to ecclesiology. I belong to a religious order that emerged out of lay communities, and have been codirector of a Center for Lay Communities. I have attended gatherings of SCCs in Paris, Santiago (Chile), and have participated in two International Theological Consultations on Small Christian Communities, organized by Rev. Robert Pelton, C.S.C., at the University of Notre Dame. I am a member of the International Academy of Practical Theology.

Dr. Jeanette Rodriguez, Seattle University. I am a U.S. Latina theologian inspired by the faith and struggle of *el pueblo*. My work in systematic theology in conjunction with my professed commitment to both Liberation and Feminist Theology directs me to place both my personal and professional commitment at the service of justice. This commitment takes the form of understanding, articulating, and offering the insights of the lived faith experience of U.S. Latinos to the larger theological enterprise. This commitment is manifested in work with leadership and involvement in U.S. Latino communities as well as those in Mexico and Central America.

Dr. Edith (Edie) Turner, University of Virginia. I am an anthropologist with a lifelong interest in the working of religion in society, mostly that of small-scale groups, whether they be in African villages, pilgrimages on the personal level, or small Christian groups. I am what William James termed a radical empiricist, and my researches have convinced me that ordinary people are experiencing religion in company with each other to an extent that has not yet been fully realized. My participant studies of ritual and symbol have necessitated the use of the term *communitas* to describe the relationship among people in liminal "betwixt-and-between" communities.

Dr. Evelyn Eaton Whitehead, Whitehead Associates. As a social scientist, my interests lie at the intersection of adult development and social psychology. Studying community settings—in religious congregations, parish life, and small faith communities—has expanded my awareness of the reciprocal ways that persons and groups shape one another. Exploring adult lives of faith has deepened my appreciation of people's hunger for both self-expression and self-transcendence. These overlapping interests have energized my participation in this small Christian community research project.

Dr. James D. Whitehead, Whitehead Associates. I am a pastoral theologian and historian of religion. My special interests are adult spirituality (especially around questions of sexuality and the role of the emotions in spiritual life) and *a spirituality for living in the world.* Collaborating with Evelyn Whitehead, I have been involved over the past twenty years in examining the changing experiences and expectations of community in the U.S. Catholic Church since Vatican II. Currently, I am returning to an earlier passion, participating in the encounter between Christian faith and the Chinese culture today.

In the formation of these two teams we have been eager to have a balance of women and men researchers and theologians, and to have the Hispanic/Latino experience well represented in both areas.

Community and Catholic

We have focused our research upon small Christian communities in the U.S. Catholic Church. While there is an extensive literature about SCCs, including those in the U.S. Catholic Church, the only serious, systematic interpretation undertaken to date is that of Rev. John Vandenakker in his book, *Small Christian Communities and the Parish*.

The formal topic for our research is small Christian communities in the U.S. Catholic Church. In the early stages of the research we discussed at length how we would handle the designations *community* and *Catholic*.

Having named the subject of our research as we did, we chose to include in our database almost all of the groups that reported in under this rubric. We were concerned not to impose our definition on the phenomenon, but to meet those who have located themselves within the phenomenon as we named it. In the section that follows, I indicate the exceptions to inclusion (and this, in fact, was a very small number of those who reported).

Community

Since our study is of communities in the U.S. Catholic Church, I will begin with a brief indication of how we approach this social unit.

We might have accepted an interpretation of community from some specific resources in sociology or anthropology. Or, we might have set limits from a particular theological understanding of community, since the word is itself a fair translation of the Greek word, *ekklesia* (which often is translated into English as *church*). We use such categories in our theological reflection on the data.

Our research interest is in the sort of community that meets often enough to create a relational texture that provides a context within which people find their faith and lived experience interacting. Therefore, we made a decision to focus our study on groups that met at least monthly. Actually, few of those who reported in met less often than monthly. Three-fourths met weekly or biweekly.

We also decided that in addition to self-identification as an SCC and meeting frequency, criteria for inclusion in the study would include only groups that regularly engage in prayer, the reading and discussion of scripture, and faith sharing.

While we have included all of the communities that reported in because they understand themselves as community, in our theological reflection on the data, we will make some distinctions. We have some presuppositions about community that did not affect our count, but will come into play as we interpret the data. For example, in their book, *Community of Faith: Crafting Christian Communities Today*, Evelyn and James Whitehead propose a model from sociology (pp.18–22). In a primary group the relationship among members is the primary bonding element and conditions their shared activities. The members of a secondary group gather because they have some task or activity in common: faculty at the same school, members of a soccer team. The relationships may also have some importance, but they are not the primary reason the group gathers.

The Whiteheads suggest that a Christian community is a hybrid group: It has some characteristics of both primary and secondary groups. It may tilt one way more than the other. There may be shifts in emphasis in a community's life. But its gathering is grounded in both relational and shared task or activity commitments. The distinction between primary and secondary groups is a useful interpretive typology. Communities and groups move back and forth in their configuration; the intensity of one reason or another for gathering varies in a community's life. We are talking about something that more closely resembles a continuum than two utterly discrete types of groups.

In a similar vein, theologians sometimes insist that a Christian community is always both gathered and sent. Members attend to each other within the group, and are at least minimally willing to provide mutual support and to endure discomfort in order to address conflict when it arises. They also care about the condition of the world outside the group and respond with acts of mercy (providing resources) and/or acts of justice (addressing dysfunctional social systems). These theological categories are similar but not identical to the typology of primary and secondary groups.

While we affirm an important distinction between small groups that aren't community and those that are, we also recognize that a group's dynamics and rationale can and often do develop. The sort of community in which the nurturing of relationships is effective is much appreciated by most SCCs. While the maintenance of healthy human relationships is never easy, the attraction to form such groups is culturally *in*, as Robert Wuthnow's studies have demonstrated. Four out of every ten Americans belong to some kind of small group. In fact, belonging to voluntary associations has long characterized the behavior of Americans.

However, social commitment is also a strong piece of the U.S. Catholic heritage. Catholic commitments to hospitals, orphanages, and social services are such a part of the heritage backdrop that social concern is likely to condition Catholic groups sooner or later. Sometimes it emerges a little later in an SCC's life, after relationships are established.

Catholic Identity

While it would have been legitimate to take in the U.S. Catholic Church narrowly as an institutional connection or broadly as any gathering of the baptized for reasons of faith, we chose to include whoever understood themselves to be a small Christian community located somehow within Catholic culture. As you will see when we examine data on the attitudes of SCC members toward church, there is a considerable range of views about, and attachment to, the Catholic Church.

Locating the Communities

As we explored what a research project might look like, the obvious first question was: How can we find these small Christian communities? We contacted all of the organizations of which we were aware who network SCCs or have materials in which SCCs are interested (and therefore have mailing lists). We invited them to a meeting in Marriottsville, Maryland, in January 1995, immediately following the national meeting of Buena Vista. These people have provided extensive help with their membership lists and their own networks of contacts.

Our sampling is limited to SCCs in the continental, contiguous United States, though this is not the result of a conscious decision. The Charismatic Directory does list prayer groups in Hawaii and

Alaska. We also found other evidence of SCC activity in these states. They are omitted, however, only because none came into our sample frames. None responded to notices we ran in the *National Catholic Reporter*, the *Call to Action Newsletter*, *Sojourners*, and so forth.

I would like to identify the people and organizations that assembled at this first gathering. Their interest and support, their world of contacts and information, and their wisdom about the research proved invaluable. (A # identifies research team members; an * identifies theologian team members.)

Sr. Donna Ciangio, O.P., National Pastoral Life Center, New York, N.Y.

Ms. Joan Cunningham, North American Forum for Small Christian Communities, Louisville, Ky.

Ms. Martha D'Anna, Marianist Lay Network of North America, Dayton, Ohio

#Dr. William V. D'Antonio, Catholic University of America, Washington, D.C.

Mr. Reynolds Ekstrom, Loyola Pastoral Life Center, New Orleans, La.

Sr. Maria Elena Gonzales, R.S.M., Mexican American Cultural Center, San Antonio, Tex.

Ms. Kathy North Danielson, Ministry Center for Catholic Community, Seattle, Wash.

Ms. Rosalie Hartman, North American Forum for Small Christian Communities, Milwaukee, Wis.

Sr. Maureen Healy, O.S.U., *Communitas*, Washington, D.C.

#Dr. Dean Hoge, Catholic University of America, Washington, D.C.

#Dr. Guillermina Jasso, New York University, New York, N.Y.

*Dr. Patricia O'Connell Killen, Pacific Lutheran University, Yakima, Wash.

Msgr. Thomas Kleissler, International Office of Renew, Plainfield, N.J.

*Dr. Bernard J. Lee, S.M., Loyola Institute for Ministry, New Orleans, La.

#Dr. John McCarthy, Catholic University of America, Washington, D.C.

Bro. Robert Moriarty, Hartford Pastoral Office of Small Christian Communities, Bloomfield, Conn.

Ms. Nora Petersen, Buena Vista Network, Oakland, Calif.

Ms. Carrie Piro, National Alliance of Parishes Restructuring into Small Communities, Troy, Mich.

*Dr. Jeanette Rodriguez, Seattle University, Seattle, Wash.

#Dr. Edith Turner, Anthropology, University of Virginia, Charlottesville, Va.

*Dr. Evelyn Eaton Whitehead, Whitehead Associates, South Bend, Ind.

*Dr. James D. Whitehead, Whitehead Associates, South Bend, Ind.

*Dr. Virgilio Elizondo (who was not able to be present for the meeting but is a team member), San Antonio, Tex.

In addition to the contacts facilitated by the above meeting, we were able to gain additional access through the NCCB Office of Hispanic Affairs. Walter Matthews, director of Chariscenter (charismatic communities), provided us with 1992 and 1997 directories, listing 5,100 charismatic communities. We had notices in the *National Catholic Reporter, Pace, Sojourners,* and the *Call to Action Newsletter,* to catch communities that were not members of any of the above organizations or networks. We also included two smaller organizations: the St. Boniface Cell model from Pembroke Pines, Florida, and the SINE model that was developed by Fr. Alfonso Navarro in Mexico, and is gradually making its way into the United States.

The research teams were also aware of the existence of a number of groups known nationally as Intentional Eucharistic Communities. They identify themselves as small Christian communities, even though their individual membership numbers were reported to run as high as 200 to 500. These communities often have smaller groupings within them (committees, prayer groups, action groups). The research team agreed that these could qualify as small communities if our other criteria were met: that the groups meet at least monthly, that they identify themselves as SCCs, and that they engage in prayer, reflection on scripture, and faith sharing.

We sampled college and university campus experience (Catholic, private, and public) through Catholic campus ministry contacts. We mailed the census survey to about a fourth of the total number of campus ministry contacts we had available (289 mailings), with 105 returns. The return rate of 36 percent was lower than we had hoped for. In addition to census survey information, campus communities were included in the motivations survey but not the attitudes survey (it was too late in the academic year to get returns). While we have gathered some information about the campus SCCs, it is not as extensive as for the other SCC types, so I have not included them in the report. You will find a summary of campus SCCs in the appendices. It is certainly our judgment that this is an important form of SCC life since young adults do not constitute a large percentage of all the other kinds of SCC groups.

We were also aware, through limited contact and hearsay, of SCCs composed entirely of women. Some communities with a women-only membership are included in our census and samples, but we do not know whether this configuration was a deliberate choice based on women's issues. Our efforts to locate the women's groups who are women-only by deliberate choice had limited success. Many of them are not interested in publicity, only in *getting on with it*. Since our gathering of data was completed, Sheila Durkin Dierks' book, *Women Eucharist*, has been published. She has located about 100 women's communities that "celebrate Eucharist without inviting or including a priest to act as presider or celebrant" (p. 15). I spoke with her after the book's publication, learning that she too did not find it easy to locate women's communities. While we know, therefore, that there are SCCs composed entirely of women by choice, they are not included in our reporting because we do not have sufficient data to support reliable interpretation.

We also know that SCCs exist as lay communities associated with religious orders of women and men. Our inquiries did not generate any kind of workable list of communities from which we could gather data. Since that time an organization has come into existence called the North American Conference of Associates and Religious, with a quarterly publication, *The Associate*. Jean Sonnenberg, the editor, put me in touch with a 1994–95 research project conducted by Srs. Louis Hembrecht and Paul Rae Rose. Questionnaires were sent to 381 communities of women religious. The research found some 14,500 associate members. Sonnenberg senses that the majority of these meet the criteria for being SCCs, a judgment that has not been empirically verified. We have not, therefore, been able to include associate communities, most of which are composed of both lay and religious, in our database. We are not aware of any organized data concerning associate members of communities of religious men, although we know in fact that some exist. (I am aware, for example, of a large network of lay Marianist communities with national and regional structures.)

Stage One: The Census and Subsequent Grouping

The first stage of the research was to sample the communities we were able to contact in view of the above connections. We wanted to know basics about who the people were who belonged to SCCs, what they did, why they did it, and what they perceived the impact to be. The various kinds of lists provided by the several organizations meant that a multiple stage sampling process would be required for us to gain some idea of the extent of SCC growth.

For their part, The North American Forum for Small Christian Communities provided us with the names of their contact persons in the forty-five dioceses in which they were working to develop SCCs. (The number of dioceses with which the North American Forum is affiliated numbered 64 as of fall 1997). We found that some dioceses were highly organized and able to provide us with the names and addresses of the contact persons in all the parishes in which SCC activity was taking place. Through them we were able to gain an esti-mate of the number of SCCs within each parish.

The National Alliance of Parishes Restructuring into Com-munities (Rev. Art Baranowski's organization) provided us with the names of the pastors of all the parishes that had participated in his workshops. By 1995, he had organized workshops in some 60 dio-ceses, with participation by some 700 parishes. We drew a one-in-four sample of parishes, and with letters and questionnaires, found that about 60 percent of the parishes that had participated in these workshops had followed up with one or more SCCs.

It seemed plausible that some SCCs modeled on Father Bara-nowski's ideas as contained in his writings might well exist outside the procedure we were employing. However, given the importance Father Baranowski placed on the role of the parish pastor in the early stages of SCC development, the use of the parish lists based on the workshops promised us the best access to this type of SCC.

Buena Vista is a voluntary membership association, and at the time of the Stage One activity, it numbered some 450 paid members. We did a 25 percent sample, again taking into account the geographical distribution of the membership. We found that 90 percent of Buena Vista members belonged to an SCC. Some were derived from Post-RENEW, some related to North American Forum activity, and some clearly were the result of local parish lay and priest initiatives.

Working with the leaders noted above, with the benefit of word of mouth, and with the responses to our media requests, we slowly developed a census questionnaire that became the primary data-gathering instrument for the first stage of this project. This questionnaire was prepared through extensive consultation between the two teams, modified through conference discussion, pretested, revised on the basis of pretesting, and finally prepared for formal usage. It was designed to provide basics about the people who are members of SCCs, what they do when they gather, the degree and structure of formal leadership, contacts through parishes or other organizations, and their activities when they meet.

Perhaps the most important finding in this first stage was the apparent size and dynamic growth of SCCs in almost all parts of the country. Some dioceses had more than 100 parishes with SCC activity, and some parishes had as many as 50 or more active SCCs. More than 3.5 million Catholics had participated in RENEW, creating some 350,000 small groups, and were now being encouraged to move into a Post-RENEW process, often in collaboration with the North American Forum for Small Christian Communities. Only the Call to Action and ECC SCCs numbered 100 or fewer each.

Based upon similarities disclosed in the census survey, we classified SCCs in groupings that will be used throughout this book. These are, of course, generalizations. When data are presented, it does not mean that every SCC in a particular grouping conforms to all parts of the generalized description, only that those communities included in a grouping, *for the most part*, have many of the same characteristics.

1. GSC: the Broad General (Type of) Small Christian Community

We decided that for purposes of the larger study, we could create one major subtype by combining the communities about which we gathered data from the following sources: Buena Vista, the North American Forum for Small Christian Communities, The National Alliance of Parishes Restructuring into Communities, Post-RENEW, and some of the responses to notices in traditional Catholic print media. Although we group these communities for the report that follows, the responses are coded so that we can separate and compare them. The differences among them, however, are minor.

It is not difficult to understand why these organizations exhibit notable similarities. The national leaders all know each other and have often worked together, sometimes sitting on each other's boards of directors. The groups are similar in size, have regular weekly or biweekly meetings, and follow an orderly routine of prayer, scripture reading and discussion with focused questions, and faith sharing. What we had not fully anticipated was how closely they matched up in age, gender, and education. Most of these SCCs are parish-based. The GSC type comprises about 24,000 SCCs, about 65 percent of those we have researched. Since they are two-thirds of the total, they will be the major focus.

2. H/L: Hispanic/Latino Communities

There are at least 7,500 Hispanic-Latino communities. Membership is almost entirely Hispanic/Latino, whereas membership in the GSC communities is almost entire Anglo.

Gathering data on the growth of SCCs among the growing Hispanic/Latino population of the United States was somewhat complicated. We found charismatic Latino prayer groups, especially in California and the Southwest. We found groups that had emerged out of RENEW and out of Buena Vista and North American Forum activity. We also found SCCs that had formed as a result of workshops given by Fr. Alfonso Navarro, with the appellation SINE (Systematic Integral New Evangelization). Some SCCs are derived from the Latin American model. Others owe their existence to priests and religious women who have taken it upon themselves to develop SCCs within the Latino population. Largely through workshops and courses sponsored by the Mexican American Cultural Center in San Antonio, the Brazilian theologian, Rev. José Marins, has had a marked influence on many Hispanic/Latino SCCs in Texas.

As far back as 1986–87, the U.S. bishops had made a commitment to help foster the growth of SCCs within the Latino populations. Finally, in January 1996, the bishops formally approved a publication detailing a program for the growth of small church communities. The Office of Hispanic Affairs of the National Council of Catholic Bishops has responsibility for overseeing their growth throughout dioceses that have any significant number of Latinos in the population.

The census data showed significant differences between Latino SCC members and the others, especially in matters of age, education, and income, as well as in the focus of their gatherings. This data, in addition to the special attention being given them by the NCCB Office of Hispanic Affairs, convinced us to designate the Hispanic/Latino SCCs as a special type.

The 7,500 H/L SCCs constitute about 20 percent of the SCCs we have researched. H/L and GSC together represent 85 percent of the total.

3. Chr: Charismatic Communities

The directories that Chariscenter provided indicated communities organized by diocese, with the name and address of the liaison person for each diocese. At least 4,800 SCCs are charismatic. The 1992 directory listed some 5,141 prayer groups in just about every diocese of the country, and indicated that these groups averaged about 20 members each. Chariscenter was the only organization with such complete and detailed information.

Based upon our sampling of the 1992 directory, we estimate that about 4,800 currently function as communities, constituting about 13 percent of the SCCs we have researched. The 1997 directory listed 4,860 prayer groups.

4. CTA/ECC: Call to Action and Eucharist Centered Communities

CTA communities are those we contacted through a Call to Action directory of SCCs, or at the annual CTA convention. Some

CTA communities have emerged in the past few years primarily in response to the national Call to Action organization, centered in Chicago. However, it should be noted that there is no necessary tie between the emerging groups around the country and the CTA office in Chicago beyond the willingness of the central office to include the local groups in the national directory upon request. We mailed census questionnaires to all the groups listed in either the 1995 or 1996 CTA directory, 94 of whom responded to the survey. Though CTA is the basis of contact with these communities, the CTA designation does not imply that all community members belong to the CTA.

The most obvious defining characteristic of ECCs is that Eucharist is regularly celebrated when the groups gather. These communities are not parish-connected. Average membership tends to be larger than in any of the other SCC groups, with size ranging from as low as 15 to as large as several hundred. There is no formal organization that links ECCs, although *Communitas*, an ECC in the Washington D.C. area, sponsored a national gathering of ECCs and is, perhaps, loosely a point of identification.

Although differences exist, there are many similarities between the two groups that justify combining them. Both CTA and ECC communities have a more highly educated and affluent membership than the typical Catholic SCC. Both show larger social awareness, are more apt to act upon social commitment than the typical SCC group, and are more likely to identify themselves as liberal. Both groups tend to be outspoken about what is perceived as positive *and* negative regarding the church.

We know of less than 100 communities in each of these groups. Together the CTA/ECC communities constitute less than 1 percent of the SCCs we have researched.

A Word on Sampling

In Stages Two and Three of the research, we *sampled* the general SCC population to inquire about members' motivations and attitudes. A word on sampling will be helpful for those less familiar with empirical research.

Many people in the United States are familiar with research and with predictions based on research, because they hear, read, and see it on television at election time. Indeed, with polling being such a standard part of our daily lives, readers of newspapers and news magazines can expect to see somewhere in a polling article a statement telling them the size of the sample obtained and the probable margin of error in that particular poll.

Sampling is a way of studying a particular population by systematically choosing a small percentage of it and making inferences for the entire population. A sample is *random* or *representative* if it accurately reflects the characteristics of the population being studied.

We subdivided the church's approximately 180 dioceses into eight geographic regions (following the 1993 *Kenedy Catholic Directory)* and sampled one diocese within each region (for all parts of the study we have information region by region, although it will not be reported in that detailed way here). The eight regions and the dioceses selected are as follows:

1. Northeast   Manchester, N.H.
2. Mid-Atlantic   Pittsburgh, Pa.
3. Southeast   Charlotte, N.C.
4. North Central   Youngstown, Ohio
5. Southwest   Ft. Worth, Tex.
6. Midwest   Dubuque, Iowa
7. Mountain   Las Cruces, N.Mex.
8. Pacific   Fresno, Calif.

Our early efforts showed that SCCs were to be found in all parts of the country, and in some cases seemed to be in a dynamic stage of growth. For the motivations survey and the attitudes survey, we devised a sampling technique that was as representative as possible, considering the open-ended nature of the SCC movement. New groups were regularly coming into existence even as we were sampling. For example, while our research was going on, Fr. Art Baranowski conducted workshops for the development of parish-based communities in places as disparate as Bismarck, North Dakota; Columbus, Ohio; Tulsa, Oklahoma; and Jackson, Mississippi.

Stage Two: Motivations Survey

From the motivations survey we wanted to learn why people joined SCCs, what impact it had on their lives and on the church, and whether their reasons for continuing to be members were different from their original reasons for joining.

Stage Three: Attitudes Survey

From the attitudes survey we wanted to learn what people believed and/or felt about the church and the world on a range of issues, and whether they considered themselves conservative, moderate, or liberal in religious and political matters.

In both the motivations and attitudes surveys we were interested in knowing how gender, age, education, and church-related activities impacted motivations and behaviors. The report in this book selects from the huge amount of data at our disposal.

We created two separate samples for these two surveys, drawing from all eight regions so as not to burden any single SCC group with more than one survey. With both surveys we aimed for a 50 percent response, which would yield between 90 and 100 responses from each type. We achieved this rate with all parts except for the Hispanic/Latino communities in the attitudes survey, which came in at only 7 percent. While that percentage is too small to provide the same degree of probability as the other parts of the survey, the data still help to draw some kind of picture. In the chapters that follow, whenever the H/L is accompanied with an asterisk, H/L*, that indicates the smaller return on the attitudes survey.

To carry out the objectives of Stages Two and Three, we began by drawing a sample of U.S. dioceses. This we did, as I indicated above, by dividing the country into eight regions and then sampling a diocese in each region.

Once having selected the eight dioceses for study, the next step was to determine how many SCCs by type were already known to exist within these dioceses. This is what we knew:

(1) the number of charismatic prayer groups, with addresses by parish;

(2) the names and addresses of Buena Vista members within particular dioceses;

(3) the location and contact persons for all known CTA and ECC groups within the dioceses;

(4) the contact persons for known GSC and H/L groups within the dioceses.

Given the fact that some dioceses did not have known groups of several of the types, we had to resort to a number of sampling techniques to achieve as representative a national sample as possible. To illustrate the problem and how we handled it, we cite the case of CTA and ECC. If there was no CTA or ECC group in one of the eight dioceses in the national sample, we drew from the CTAs and/or ECCs that did exist in that particular region (e.g., New England), a sample of the groups needed to ensure representation. We made use of phone contacts, interviews, and other networking to seek out SCCs of all types.

Where a diocese had a North American Forum office, we contacted the head person, learned what that person knew about all aspects of SCC activity within parishes, and built our lists for sampling from that information.

In dioceses that did not have a North American Forum office, we used the *Kenedy Catholic Directory* to obtain a list of all parishes in the diocese. We then sampled parishes, again using random numbers, and telephoning the pastor or person designated by the pastor to obtain the desired information about SCC activity within the parish.

An updated Buena Vista mailing list informed us of its members who lived in the eight dioceses. The National Alliance of Parishes Restructuring into Communities lists informed us of parishes in the dioceses that had participated in Baranowski workshops.

The Chariscenter Directory provided contact persons for each of the eight dioceses. In some but not all of the dioceses there were people working specifically on the development of SCCs within the Hispanic-Latino population, so they became the contact source.

We had the CTA Directory to help us locate SCCs with some CTA connection; as expected, less than half the dioceses had CTA communities; the same was true of ECCs. Since we had the entire national list for both of them, we had to resort to sampling within regions for each of those two lists.

The questionnaires used in the motivations and attitudes surveys developed from a three-day meeting of the sociologists with the theologians, followed by numerous faxes and phone calls, as theologians and sociologists sought to ensure that the information desired could be obtained by the questions asked. Both surveys were translated into Spanish.

Stage Four: National Survey of U.S. Roman Catholics

To be able to interpret the SCC experience in the U.S. Catholic Church, it is useful to know how SCC members compare and contrast with the general Catholic population. We therefore contracted the services of the University of Maryland Survey Research Center to carry out an attitudes survey on a representative national sample of the Catholic population aged 18 and over, and also included those who said they were formerly Catholic. The size of the national sample was 802, with 167 (17 percent) made up of former Catholics. We modified the attitudes survey used with SCCs so as to gather information about why former Catholics left the church, and what their current religious practices were.

We were able to distinguish between Catholics who belonged to a religious or church-related small group within the last ten years and those who had not. In the pages that follow, the abbreviation GRC/NG refers to those Catholics who have not been members of a small group in the last ten years (60 percent of the Catholics in the sample).

Stage Five: Direct Contact with Communities and with Individual Members

The final part of the data-gathering activity involved participant and nonparticipant observation of SCC gatherings and interviews with SCC leaders and members. To carry this out over a four-month period, we employed five persons more or less intensively, and two others in special situations. We coordinated our efforts to observe and interview SCCs of each of the six types. This required travel in all eight regions of the country, including seven of the eight dioceses in the diocesan sample. However, conflicts with meeting dates and travel schedules prevented us from completing any interviews or observations in the Manchester diocese. A total of more than 80 observations and interviews were carried out, with an average of 13 per SCC type, and 16 of the GSC type (since that is by far the largest group). We have transcriptions of entire community meetings and of interviews with individual community members.

Once again, the format that all interviewers used was the product of protracted interaction between the theological team and the researchers. Dr. D'Antonio held a training session in Washington, D.C., for those who would conduct the interviews.

Research: Its Scope and Limitations

The census survey, the SCC attitudes and motivations surveys, and the survey of the general Catholic population provide us with very extensive quantitative data. Our direct contacts with communities do indeed tell the same story as the quantitative data, but with names and faces, feelings and configurations. Throughout this report, you will hear these voices. These multiple research methodologies frame the scope of what we have learned about small Christian communities in the U.S. Catholic Church.

I am also aware that what we know is selective from all there is to know, and that while interpretation places information in a stronger light, it also *massages* it into the shapes of the interpreters' models. No apologies for that. It's how we learn.

> Floundering through mere happenings
> and then concocting accounts of how they hang together
> is what knowledge and allusion alike consist in.
> Clifford Geertz, 1995, 3

I have long believed with Friedrich Nietzsche that there is no such thing as an uninterpreted fact. I am further convinced by the hermeneutical tradition that every interpretation of a fact has some free construction in it from the interpreter, which he or she can rarely detect because it just looks like the true insides of a fact. I think it healthy for theologians and social scientists to acknowledge this up front.

A phenomenon exists in the Catholic Church around the world of people (largely laypeople) gathering into small groups and meeting with some regularity, usually to discuss scripture and life. That we have not settled upon a way of naming these groups shows their slippery nature. They *are* called faith communities, faith groups, faith sharing groups, base communities, basic Christian communities, basic ecclesial communities, house churches, small Christian communities, small church communities, intentional Christian communities, intentional eucharistic communities, charismatic communities, and so forth. The Reverend Joseph Healy, a Maryknoll missioner in Africa, has collected over a thousand ways of labeling these groups.

I was aware from early on how different were the theological, sociological, and anthropological takes on this phenomenon, and how different were the questions we thought of putting to it. I think it useful, perhaps, at the close of this chapter that describes our research, to reflect briefly on what it is we understand ourselves to be doing. I rely heavily on conversations with my colleague, Dr. William D'Antonio, with his written comments in Appendix II, and with some reflections from a recent book by renowned anthropologist, Clifford Geertz, entitled *After the Fact*.

Sociology joins the other sciences in developing its hypotheses, generalizations, and theories on the basis of empirical research. An hypothesis is a statement of a relationship between variables (such as between education and attitudes toward social issues) that is capable of being verified or denied by empirical observation.

We began with direct awareness of small groups of Catholics, gathering with some regularity, who perceive themselves as communities. We experienced them as they attended gatherings such as Buena Vista or the two national congresses. We perceived them to be numerous enough to gain some national attention, for example, in periodicals such as the *National Catholic Reporter*. But we had no way of guessing at their numbers. We also hypothesized from our nonsystematic contacts with them that people joined them because they had needs and desires that were not being met in traditional parish life.

Our census work helped us locate and contact groups that considered themselves to be small Christian communities. Our contacts with organizations provided us with extensive mailing lists (such as those from Buena Vista or from Chariscenter). We did random sampling, and then extrapolated, based on the statistical probability that our sample was representative of the whole group.

The focus of the census survey was on the particular SCCs, not on individual members. In the attitudes and motivations surveys we gather more precise information about members of communities (e.g., Mass attendance, education, income, and so forth). Because we have control data from other empirical studies, we can say, for example, that regular Sunday Mass attendance among SCC members is higher than for the general Catholic population, and that except for Hispanic/Latino communities, SCC members tend to be better educated and more affluent than the average U.S. Catholic. These are generalizations based upon comparative empirical data.

There is a lot of freedom in the kind of information one seeks from the groups, once they have been identified. No empirical reading, therefore, is purely objective. Questions other than those we asked would have provided different information, and a different (though probably not conflicting) profile. The questions we put to the communities represent the collective interests of the two teams working on the research, and collective judgment about what we deemed important to learn. Given research and theological specializations, interests differ. Some members, for example, were interested in how much SCC development profited from the wisdom of the tradition and what were, therefore, the principal continuities. Others were specifically interested in the innovative components and/or challenges to the traditions. Other members were especially interested in developmental questions: What changes do SCC members perceive to have occurred as a result of the SCC experience?

Another member was concerned with the religious imagination at work in any religious person, whether there were some shared characteristics among SCC members, and whether religious imagination is affected by SCC membership. While we do have some limited hints on this from our data, we finally agreed that while this would have been a very productive research direction, we lacked the time and resources to undertake something so massive.

Another interest of a particular member was how much motivation for SCC membership springs from religious reasons (e.g., to be the body of Christ more effectively), and how much originates from the growing cultural hunger for groups and community (Wuthnow, 1994). This was a difficult one to pin down. We can note, however, that religious motivations were named more often among reasons for joining an SCC than for remaining a member. Community and relational support ranks higher in reasons for staying than those for joining. The interpretation of this data is, of course, complex. Have SCCs just become support groups, as healthy as they may be, or does their religious commitment so deepen the community experience that the support they offer one another is, as Paul would have it, the way that members of the body of Christ treat each other? I think of how many admonitions in the Pauline letters are about how members of communities should be together with each other in life, because of who they are in Christ.

These latter questions lead to what might be considered a third step in empirical research: formulation of theories about the generalized conclusions. One theory could be that most Catholics join SCCs because, like four of every ten Americans, they are looking for a small group. Another could be that they are searching for a level of communal Christian life that traditional parish life alone does not provide. Our experience of what happens at SCC meetings and our interviews with SCC members give way to theoretical interpretations.

As I indicated earlier, we have used multiple instruments, fashioned through incredible interdisciplinary collaboration. We have accumulated more information than can be presented in a book such as this. I just thought it would be both honest and professional to acknowledge that what we do know is very much shaped by the interests of our two teams (especially the theologians), and by the scope and limits of research methods (especially the research team).

As we track with and interpret the phenomenon of small Christian communities in the U.S. Catholic Church, we are (in Geertz's words) building systems of discourse and formulating structures of representation, which we put forward "as assertions and arguments, dressed with evidence," convinced that we are recounting things that are indeed the case. Our intention is to describe a form of life and to present it in a certain light (Geertz, 1995, 19).

This chapter has described the research and the people engaged in it. We have acknowledged the impact of our interests and specializations on the research because no research is entirely objective. In fact, starting points make research possible. And starting points, in this context, are interchangeable with presuppositions or prejudices. We have indicated our sense of both the scope and limitations of what we do.

Theological Interpretation

If *geo-logy* is a systematic arrangement of our knowledge of the earth, and if *zoo-logy* is a systematic arrangement of our knowledge of living things, then *theo-logy* ought to be a systematic arrangement of our knowledge of God. But how we get our *database* on God differs from the other two.

We are in the world and whatever we can know about anything must have some reference to this basic location. If we can know anything about God, then God must be (and is!) present somehow in the world. The worldly appearances of God are a proper *database* for theological interpretation.

"The people of God," we read in *Gaudium et Spes* from Vatican II, "believes that it is led by the Spirit of the Lord, who fills the earth. Motivated by this faith, we labor to decipher authentic signs of God's presence and purpose in the happenings, needs, and desires in which this people has a part along with other people of our age." Our presumption is that reading God's presence and purpose in the emergence of small Christian communities is possible by deciphering what is going on in happenings, needs, and desires of the people of God involved in this movement. We do not presuppose that every happening, need, or desire is a movement of the Spirit. The unambiguous never shows up in human activities. Yet, as we confront the report on the religious hungers that move people to the generous presence needed for SCCs to happen, we do believe that the Spirit is acting within and through us. Is God speaking?

In the epilogue to *I and Thou*, Martin Buber says that people sometimes ask him why, if God once spoke so often, God doesn't seem to be speaking much anymore. Buber says the problem is that most of us expect God to speak above everyday experience, or along-side everyday experience (Buber, 1958, 136-37). So we fail to plumb everyday experience, which is where God does his talking. When the events that make up our lives call us to decision, the personal speech of God is there for the hearing. So we have to listen *through* lived experience, not above it or alongside it. Chapter five is our attempt to read the personal speech of God as those syllables are articulated in the shape of small Christian communities in the U.S. Catholic Church. A tentative reading, to be sure. But a reading.

So, here, then, is the fuller story.

3

Catholics in Small Christian Communities
Who Belongs and Why

PART ONE:
WHO BELONGS?

A Significant Minority

There are about 60,000,000 Roman Catholics in the United States. Regular participation in Sunday Eucharist is not the only church connector, but it is a valuable indicator of people's active sense of belonging. Gallup puts regular Catholic attendance at about 40 percent of all adult Catholics. The survey conducted by Hadaway, Marler, and Chaves designates attendance at 26.7 percent. The survey of the general Catholic population that we conducted places attendance at 32 percent (about midway between the other two). Our survey and the Gallup survey were conducted through phone calls. Hadaway/Marler/Chaves visited parishes in selected dioceses, tallied the parish rolls, and counted people who actually showed up for Sunday/weekend Eucharist. In round numbers, considering the different surveys, one can safely say that about a third of U.S. Catholics participate in Sunday Eucharist regularly.

At a time when Catholics are participating less in the rhythms of church life, we have vested interests in discerning why some people are doing considerably more than is normally expected: What kind of people are they, and why do they do it? Those are the two questions addressed in this chapter. Members of SCCs are not the only people doing more, but they are a clearly identifiable group that we have researched extensively.

In this part of the chapter that deals with who belongs to small Christian communities, information will be presented under three headings. Section One is basic profile information, such as numbers, gender, income, education, ethnicity, and the longevity of communities. Section Two concerns the religious values that motivate the behavior of SCC members, and Section Three addresses ideological issues and attitudes.

In some of the tables that follow, I will sometimes compare SCC members with the general Catholic population in a specific way. In the survey we had conducted by the University of Maryland, we asked those queried whether membership in a group with a religious or spiritual purpose was part of their experience. About 40 percent said yes. Since that would, of course, include SCC members, I have chosen, when I offer a comparison with the general Catholic population, to compare SCC members with Catholics who do not belong to a small group, which is about 60 percent. I remind readers that GRC/NG names the general Roman Catholic (GRC) population that does not belong to a group (NG = no group) with a religious or spiritual purpose.

Also, I will sometimes give an average figure for CTA/ECC groups, which comprise less than 1 percent of communities in our research. They are important because of their educational and financial configuration. They are the most challenging to Catholic tradition and also the most actively responsive to the church's social teaching. When the differences between CTA and ECC are quite large, I will cite both figures.

I would also note that when figures do not add up to 100 percent, there are several possible reasons. In some instances, people did not respond to an item. Occasionally, they checked more than one response to the same item. And in still other instances, there was a small reponse to disparate items, too small to weigh in as helpful information.

Table 1
Average Number of Men, Women, and Children in SCCs

Type	GSC	H/L	Chr	CTA/ECC	
Women	8	11	17	10	31
Men	5	6	10	6	30
Under 18	6	8	5	3	21

Section 1: A Basic Profile of SCC Members

Communities vary in number from several members to over 100 (see Table 1). If we look at the two largest groupings, GSC and H/L, the average number would be between 13 and 17, with 6–8 children additionally—and remember that these two groups together constitute 85 percent of the SCCs we have uncovered in our research. Keep in mind, however, that there are a few larger groups in most categories that raise the average. We know also that while charismatic communities list an average of 27 adult members, the actual attendance at prayer meetings was closer to 12, sometimes up to 20. ECC membership tends to be larger than in the other groups.

The 13–17 average of most groups means that every member normally has a chance to be interactive at each gathering. Some of the larger groups note that there are subgroups for some part of a gathering.

Women outnumber men in membership, as they do in regular church attendance. The exception is the ECC where the gender mixture is almost equal.

What is most immediately striking is that the majority of SCC members are middle-aged and above (40+): 75–80 percent for GSC, Chr, and CTAs, whereas the number of young adults (18–39) ranges between 18–25 percent for all of the groups (see Table 2). It would be helpful to compare percentages vis-à-vis young adults (18–39) and those 40 and older (see Table 3).

Of the three largest groups, the H/L communities have the highest number of young adults but the number is still less than a fourth. The meager presence of young adults needs to be a concern of SCCs as well as of the church in general.

Table 2
Age of Community Members

Age	GSC	H/L	Chr	CTA/ECC
17 or less	5%	23%	6%	15%
18–29	4	9	6	8
30–39	14	14	13	15
40–49	25	19	22	22
50–59	26	17	28	21
60–69	20	13	18	12
70+	6	5	7	5

Table 3
Percentage of Two Age Groups: 18–39 and 40 and Above

Age	GSC	H/L	Chr	CTA/ECC
18–39	18%	23%	19%	23%
40+	77	54	75	60

In his recent study of U.S. Catholics, *The Search for Common Ground,* James Davidson distinguishes three groups (cohorts) of Catholics: those who came to consciousness as Catholics before Vatican II; those who came to consciousness as Catholics during Vatican II and/or the immediate aftermath of the council; and those whose Catholic consciousness was formed without the experience of the council or the pre-conciliar church. It is this latter group that does not show up largely in SCCs today, something that needs to be on the agenda of those who believe in the value of SCC life for faith formation.

In his recent book, *Deep Symbols: Their Postmodern Effacement and Reclamation,* Edward Farley says that from the mid-1960s to the present, mainline churches "lost a good part of the coming generation of their young. For some reason, that generation, perhaps the first postmodern generation, could not enter the ecclesial collective unconscious, could not hear the grand narrative and the words of power. That loss should get our attention and summon us to a task,

Table 4
Income Levels in Each Type of Community

Income	GSC	H/L	Chr	CTA/ECC		GRC/NG
Under $20,000	12%	50%	21%	8%	7%	6%
$20–29,999	9	14	17	14	11	10
$30–49,999	25	11	22	17	32	30
$50–74,999	20	6	24	23	32	16
$75–99,999	8	—	4	12	10	9
$100,000+	20	—	5	16	7	8
Missing cases	6	19	7	9	1	21

the reenchantment of the deep symbols where the absent God can somehow be heard again" (Farley, 1996, 28).

Our data do not suggest reasons why there are rather few young adults, because we have not asked young people why they are not there. However, my reading of studies and my own contact with young adults lead me to accept Farley's judgment. I believe that SCCs are an environment where grappling with questions about God in a postmodern culture is much more likely to occur—not theoretical questions so much as God-implications for lived experience. This should appeal to young adults. One CTA member speaks for many SCCs in saying: "This is a very sacred space for us, because it's where you can come to be who you are, to voice your questions, your pains, and your joys, and that is how we listen to the word of God."

Table 4 shows the income levels of group members. For comparison, it includes a sixth column indicating the income level of general population Catholics who do not belong to any kind of small religious group.

With the exception of H/L income levels, which are predictably lower, SCC members tend to be more affluent than the general population with which we compare them. About half of GSC, CTA, and ECC members are in the income bracket of $50,000 or above, compared with about a third of the general population figure and Chr members.

It is no surprise, of course, that there is a reasonable correlation between income and education.

Table 5
Educational Level of SCC Members

Education	GSC	H/L	Chr	CTA/ECC	GRC/NG
High School or less	21%	67%	34%	12%	43%
Some College	23	14	26	15	26
College Degree	33	12	27	37	23
Graduate, Professional Degree	23	8	13	35	6

Table 6
Ethnic/Racial Composition of Communities

Ethnicity	GSC	H/L	Chr	CTA/ECC
African American	2%	—	3%	2%
Asian American	1	1	6	1
Caucasian	92	1	76	93
Hispanic/ Latino	4	98	14	4
Other	1	—	1	—

First of all, it is not surprising that H/L community members are less educated because of the number of Hispanic/Latinos who are immigrants or first generation citizens (see Table 5). What is noteworthy is that over half of the general type of SCC members and 72 percent of CTA/ECC members have bachelor or graduate degrees, compared with 29 percent of the general Catholic population. Although numerically, CTA/ECC communities are a small percentage of the total of SCCs, it will be important to take note of their basic attitudes, given that they are very educated Catholics.

The Chr communities are the most ethnically diverse, though predominantly Caucasian (see Table 6). The remainder of the communities are either largely Caucasian (over 90 percent) or, in the case of H/L, almost entirely Hispanic/Latino (98 percent). Some

Table 7
Longevity of Communities

Community Age	GSC	H/L	Chr	CTA/ECC	
Less than one year	10%	10%	3%	13%	4%
1–3 years	34	26	12	38	16
4–5 years	21	26	10	13	13
6–10 years	18	13	16	22	21
11–20 years	7	9	29	10	21
21+ years	3	4	27	4	24

reflections from the H/L interviews suggest the importance of H/L small communities in helping to preserve Hispanic/Latino cultural identity. We found very few SCCs in predominantly African American parishes.

As shown in Table 7, the two groups with the largest number of communities in existence six years or more are Chr (56 percent) and ECC (66 percent), and correspondingly the smallest number of newer groups, three years or less: Chr (15 percent) and ECC (20 percent). The greatest numbers of young groups, three years or less, are found among GSC (44 percent), H/L (36 percent), and CTA (51 percent).

It is clear where the most new activity is taking place (GSC, H/L, CTA), and where the larger numbers of older communities are to be found (Chr and ECC). Two interpretations are possible. One would be that the groups with the youngest communities are not able to keep these communities going, so there are fewer older communities. The other interpretation is that there is much more new activity; and how long they continue would remain to be seen. I think the second of these is the more likely interpretation, given the significant amount of new activity that I described in chapter one, for example, the recent increase in lectionary-based scripture guides published for SCCs.

In telephone conversations with Hispanic ministry leaders in dioceses from which we had not received responses to our mail-outs, we learned that there are at least a dozen dioceses in which the SCC movement among Hispanics has just begun. The bishops gave

Table 8
Values Identified as *Very* Important

Values	GSC	H/L	Chr	CTA/ECC		GRC/NG
Family	96%	92%	92%	97%	88%	95%
Prayer	90	89	96	89	59	66
Helping others	83	81	83	88	89	73
Spiritual matters	78	78	90	85	66	56
Parish	73	86	74	47	58	47
Environment	51	56	35	58	67	70
Bible study	39	89	77	52	13	28
Job, career	34	67	21	32	28	56
Political issues	24	25	20	32	47	26
Money	7	19	5	4	6	34
Having nice things	3	26	3	2	6	16

formal approval to the development of *small church communities* (the language they chose) in 1996. A guideline booklet has been issued, and leaders in Hispanic/Latino ministry are beginning to sow the SCC seeds.

One diocese in the northwest reports that there are 140,000 baptized persons of Hispanic/Latino origin, of which only about 10,000 are active churchgoers. Leaders are being trained in some 34 parishes, with a strong focus on ecclesiology and social justice. These parishes are exploring various SCC models to find which are the most relevant to them. As you will see in the data that follow, H/L SCCs play a significantly larger role in the religious and daily social life of H/L members than in any of the other groups.

Section 2: Religious Values and Activities

We wanted to know some of the most important values that motivated SCC members and how well membership responded to those values (see Table 8).

Table 9
Religious Activities/Practices

Activities	GSC	H/L	Chr	CTA/ECC		GRC/NG
Pray daily	78%	67%	89%	75%	47%	46%
Pray often	14	8	5	12	27	20
Pray occasionally	6	11	0	7	16	21
Rosary, novena	65	78	76	53	22	48
Reconciliation, private or communal, in last 2 yrs.	71	81	81	55	43	32
Retreat, or Day of Recollection	55	61	68	64	77	12
Attend any kind of Catholic social justice meeting	39	17	26	72	61	8

The importance of prayer and of family is towering. Spiritual matters are high. For the most part, money and having nice things get low ratings, though they are higher among H/Ls than all the other groups. This is certainly related to the fact that H/Ls are substantially in the lowest income brackets of all SCC groups. Helping others is uniformly high, but political issues is 50 percent lower in the GSCs, H/Ls, and Chrs (97 percent of the total SCCs in the research). From this, one could conclude that there is not much belief that systemic issues might improve human need.

Religious Practices

SCC religious practices reveal much about the members (Table 9). The table compares SCC members with the general Catholic population that does not belong to any kind of religious group. Across the board, SCC members pray more often and participate more frequently in traditional practices such as the rosary,

Table 10
SCC Experience as Deeply Satisfying

	GSC	H/L	Chr	CTA/ECC
Deeply satisfying	69%	93%	77%	78%

novenas, and the sacrament of reconciliation. Consistent with their patterns, CTA and ECC members are far more likely to attend meetings involving issues of social justice. Because we know from other parts of our research that H/L communities are also interested in the same issues, I would surmise that the lower H/L attendance level at social justice meetings is because these issues are usually addressed at their community gatherings.

Membership Satisfaction

> "This is a very sacred space for us, because it's where you can come to be who you are, to voice your questions, your pains, and your joys. And that is how we listen to the Word of God" (CTA).

> "We evangelize ourselves in this journey—[that] is the way it's been, because we meet people with tremendous faith, and testimony, and spirituality" (H/L).

As seen in Table 10, a majority of SCC participants say that their membership is deeply satisfying. In four of the five groups, over 75 percent express that feeling, and this includes Call to Action and charismatic groups. An especially large number of H/L members also find community experience deeply satisfying.

At a time when Catholic Church attendance has dropped, it certainly seems fruitful to see what practices have attracted Catholics not only to do more than what normal expectations would suggest, but to find doing it deeply satisfying.

It is not surprising that satisfaction is high. I have correlated two of the three values named as most highly prized with the percentage of communities that say these issues are addressed at virtually every gathering (family as a value is not compared because there

Table 11
Values and Activities Compared

Comparisons	GSC	H/L	Chr	CTA/ECC	
Prayer as a value	90%	89%	96%	89%	59%
Prayer as a regular SCC activity	92	97	100	92	80
Spiritual matters as a value	78	78	90	85	66
Spirtual matters as a regular SCC activity	58	61	75	61	59

is no corresponding SCC activity, although interviews offer much evidence of the positive impact of SCCs on family life; Table 11).

Actual prayer activity at every meeting comes very close to the way it is valued. Spirituality is lower than the value named, yet still quite significant. And there are numerous things SCCs do at every meeting that are spiritual matters besides explicit attention to the topic of spirituality.

In Table 12 the survey question asked SCC members whether it is "greatly true" that their SCC is a primary source of spirituality for them. The answer is *yes* for over a fourth of GSCs, 87 percent for H/Ls, and high (close to half) for the others. If we added on those who say the statement is "somewhat true," then virtually all SCC members would be in agreement that this was a rather important source of spiritual nourishment.

Also notable is that three-fourths of H/Ls said that SCC membership increased their sense of responsibility in parish or neighborhood, and over half said their sense of civil responsibility was also heightened. For the other groups, between 20 percent and 35 percent stated that community membership heightened their sense of social responsibility. As we will see later, heightened awareness does not translate quickly into active involvement.

Table 12
Why SCC Life Is Satisfying

Why Satisfying	GSC	H/L	Chr	CTA/ECC	
Primary source of spiritual nourishment	26%	87%	51%	43%	64%
New way of participating in parish life	48	72	34	25	44
New way of being church for me	33	76	38	54	66
Primary source of social life for me	4	50	11	2	10
New sense of responsibility for parish, neighborhood	34	74	34	20	23
New sense of responsibility for civil society	20	56	32	28	38

What stands out in this data is how central the SCC is for the Hispanic/Latino communities. Some of their reflections in the interviews capture this experience. "Because of the small Christian community, we want to stay Catholic" (H/L). "You cannot tell me that I cannot pray. You cannot tell me that I cannot evangelize. He [pastor] can tell me we cannot meet here [in the church]. O.K., that's his responsibility. [But] you cannot tell me that I cannot meet in my home to pray, to receive catechesis, and to share our lives" (H/L). "We are called not only to grow in formation of the Word of God.... We are called to change the world. We are revolutionaries" (H/L). "And now, the Word, [we] try to live it and share it. A greater commitment. And, in fact, in our communities, not only act as Catholic Christians within the church, but outward" (H/L). "So if [at church] the homily is awful, the music is lousy, and the ushers are unfriendly...and that's all they get, how do they keep going? I'm

Table 13
What Influenced Interest in SCCs

Influence	GSC	H/L	Chr	CTA/ECC	
Seeking small group	37%	33%	33%	43%	48%
Parish RENEW Program	34	34	12	6	1
Friends who are members	29	56	40	46	27
Priest or Nun	19	26	9	7	6
Retreat experience	9	37	18	10	2
Conversion experience	12	47	45	15	11
Contact w/rel. community	14	31	19	20	15

not sure. But [when] you have your small communities, that's where church happens. You know that it is your church. Somehow you go to the temple once a week to worship, and this is your church, and that's a whole big difference" (H/L). While the SCC is an important experience for the great majority of community members, it plays a far larger role in Hispanic/Latino life than it does elsewhere.

I would like to point to three items in particular (see Table 13). Among the GSC and H/L communities, which comprise 85 percent of the total, the RENEW experience triggered interest in the SCC for 34 percent. The *magic* is simple in RENEW: people gather, reflect on their faith aloud together, and build relationships in the course of the program.

Second, personal contact from friends, priests, or religious is important. If we want SCCs to continue to grow, personal invitation is the most effective means of recruitment.

Third, the desire for belonging to a small group is important (for about a third of GSC, H/L, Chr). This is interesting in the light of how individualism as a towering feature of U.S. culture both makes us wary of the kinds of commitment that community requires and intensifies our need for the very thing we fear. *Habits of the Heart* has

Table 14
Weekly Eucharist

	GSC	H/L	Chr	CTA/ECC		GRC/NG
Weekly Eucharist	93%	88%	96%	66%	68%	32%

documented this double feature of our experience. Robert Wuthnow's book, *Sharing the Journey*, reports upon the propensity of Americans to join support groups as a search for the experience of community. Four out of every ten Americans belong to some kind of small group. Joining voluntary associations is not, of course, a new phenomenon. What may be new is that hunger for community is a growing motivation.

SCCs and the Institutional Church

A cluster of items helps us understand the relationship of communities and community members to the institutional Catholic Church. We wanted to know how many SCCs are connected to the church in some way, how members become active, and so forth.

Sunday Mass

Clearly, SCC members are churchgoing Catholics, while only 32 percent of the general Catholic population participates regularly in Sunday Eucharist (see Table 14).

The contrast between GSC, H/L, and Chr (97 percent of SCCs) patterns of weekly Eucharist and that of the general Catholic population which does not belong to any group (60 percent of Catholics) is remarkable. SCC members are actively present to the ritual rhythm of Catholic life. Of the different SCC types, weekly Eucharist is lower among the CTA/ECC communities but still more than double the attendance of GRC/NGs. Although in some instances, the SCC community is the only place where church is experienced, in the vast majority of cases SCC community gatherings are in addition to weekly Eucharist in the parish. These are *connected* people.

Table 15
Church Connected or Independent

Connection (or not)	GSC	H/L	Chr	CTA/ECC	
Parish	81%	91%	69%	49%	17%
Religious Order	2	1	1	6	4
Independent	11	7	14	28	65
Other	6	1	15	17	14

Institutional Connections

What is noteworthy in Table 15 is the large number of SCCs that have some kind of connection with the parish—the two largest groups: GSC at 81 percent and H/L at 91 percent. Many Chr communities are connected to the national charismatic movement. The fact that 96 percent of Chrs participate in weekly Eucharist (the highest of any group) indicates their parish affiliation, even if that is not their community connection.

We have learned since our project was completed that some research has been done, though not comprehensively, on associate communities related to religious orders. One study estimates a membership in these communities of about 14,500. But we have no data on them. This association, however, is an institutional connection.

Parish Life Ministries

Involvement in various parish ministries is one of the most palpable indications of active Catholic life. We chose four kinds of ministry participation that are commonplace in parish life today (Table 16).

What is immediately obvious is that SCC members are much more involved in typical ministries as those named here than Catholics who do not belong to any kind of small group with a religious orientation (60 percent of the total Catholic population). The CTA/ECC communities, which are the best educated and most critical, have the highest percentage of members among eucharistic ministers and lectors. This is particularly noteworthy since some

Table 16
Participation in Parish Life

Kind of Participation	GSC	H/L*	Chr	CTA/ECC		GRC/NG
Eucharistic minister	44%	36%	49%	61%	61%	6%
Lector	32	22	27	48	63	0
Usher	26	14	21	19	31	0
RENEW participation	52	44	44	46	18	2

*Asterisk indicates a smaller return on the attitudes survey.

members of the institutional church have been harshly critical of the faithfulness of CTA Catholics. When asked what triggered interest in belonging to an SCC, RENEW was mentioned more than any other SCC organization or network. RENEW offered a small group experience that many wished to continue after the RENEW program was completed.

Commitment to Being Church

The way we gathered information makes it possible for us to interpret the data in respect to gender, income, age, education, and sometimes church participation practices. Each sheds some particular light on the issue. Age control, for example, clarifies the difference between pre-Vatican II and post-Vatican II Catholics. In Table 17 I am reporting in terms of education (high school or less, some college, and college degree or more), that we deem to be important, given the rising educational level of U.S. Catholics.

H/L is not included because the sample was too small when broken down with education controls.

In the GSC and Chr communities (78 percent of the total), church membership commitment is noticeably higher than it is for the general group of Catholics who do not belong to a small religious group. Except for Chr community members, education is possibly a

Table 17
Church Membership Commitment

	GSC			Chr			CTA		
	HS	SC	CO	HS	SC	CO	HS	SC	CO
Never leave the church	79%	50%	54%	71%	88%	79%	57%	46%	39%
Might leave the church	5	10	12	6	0	3	29	25	14

	ECC			GRC/NG		
	HS	SC	CO	HS	SC	CO
Never leave the church	*	16%	23%	63%	51%	37%
Might leave the church	*	58	39	25	21	24

*The number of high school only or less in this category is negligible.

significant influence upon whether or not someone would consider leaving the church.

Magisterium and Conscience

It is no secret that there is tension among contemporary Catholics concerning the magisterium and their own personal experience or individual conscience. We asked SCC members where they stood, and we also asked this question in our general survey of Roman Catholics (see Table 18). (I will continue to compare SCC Catholics with Catholics who are not members of a religious group.) We asked what happened when a choice had to made whether to favor the pope (church teaching) or conscience (experience). The controls here include high school or less, some college, and college degree or more.

The two largest groups, GSC and Chr, are considerably higher in the tilt toward pope and church than the general Catholic population. Perhaps the item most eliciting attention is that, with

Table 18
Pope, Church Teaching/Conscience, Experience

	GSC			Chr			CTA		
	HS	SC	CO	HS	SC	CO	HS	SC	CO
Pope [church]	50%	33%	25%	72%	100%	78%	50%	32%	4%
Conscience [experience]	41	49	68	2	—	22	50	64	89

	ECC			GRC/NG		
	HS	SC	CO	HS	SC	CO
Pope [church]	50%	9%	1%	17%	13%	15%
Conscience [experience]	50	91	99	69	78	77

When the numbers do not add up to 100 percent, the reason is that some people did not answer or indicated they were unsure.

the exception of Chrs, there is a correlation between more education and a pronounced slant toward one's own conscience and experience. Once again, we must be careful not to make an exact connection between correlation and causation. But there is reason to see some connection. Higher education generally, and certainly university graduate education, encourages independent and critical thinking. Of course, this does not mean that everyone does it well. But a critical mind tends to expect that formal authority, whether civil or religious, will be corroborated with material authority—that the reasons for the formal position will be grounded evidence, reason, and/or scholarship. Generally speaking, Catholics are an educated group within U.S. culture and increasingly in the area of religion. There are two-to-three times more lay Catholics enrolled in graduate programs in theology, ministry, and religious studies than there are seminarians in the four years of theology preparatory to ordination. It is important for us as church to develop effective pastoral responses to the need of U.S. Catholics to understand the material authority that grounds formal authority.

Chr community members are the most pronounced in their tilt toward the pope and church teaching. Their attitudes are reflected in the interviews. "The way it has affected my being Catholic is what I have come to know to be the truth through my love and the church documents and church teaching" (Chr). "My attitude is that he [the pope] is a prophet. He is the prophet of our time.... I have always looked at the pope as somebody that I need to respect and listen to. But since I began in the renewal he is somebody that I really admire. I think we had better be listening to what he says, because I think that what he is saying is directly from God" (Chr).

From their tendency to think independently and critically, the strong slant toward conscience/personal experience is not surprising for the CTA/ECC communities. Their critical posture is also frequently linked with commitment to Catholicism. "I am a convert. I chose the Catholic Church in my college days, and you can't unbaptize me. I am a Catholic person by choice. So no matter if it was the pope himself saying to me: 'You're a schismatic.' I would say: 'Schismatic is a breaking of something. I have broken with no one. You have chosen to say that you are distancing from me. But I am still part of who you are, and there is still room for you in my church. I am still Catholic, strongly, deeply desirable'" (ECC).

While the CTA/ECC communities are a small percentage of the total of SCCs, they are among the most educated Catholics in the country and the most deeply committed to the church's teaching on social justice. About 98 percent have some college, and about half have graduate degrees.

Ideological Location of SCC Members

In popular usage the word *ideology* often has pejorative meanings, a political orientation with which we disagree. But technically, ideology describes the basic framework that *every* person has: our deeply held convictions, our values, the vantage point from which we see whatever we see. It is a neutral word for a person's basic beliefs. That is the meaning intended in the data tables that follow. We asked for people to designate themselves as conservative, moderate, or liberal without specifying any content.

The following tables report the data with education as the control factor.

In comparison with Catholics who do not and have not belonged to a small religious group, CTA and (especially) ECC communities are predictably far more liberal both religiously and politically (Table 19). Chr communities tend to be more conservative, both religiously and politically. A fairly consistent parallel exists between religious and political ideology.

While there are some differences, there are no glaring ones between the GRC/NG Catholics and the GSC community members (the largest of the SCC groups).

Having a Voice in the Church

We questioned SCC members and the general Catholic population on whether they felt that Catholics should have a voice in deciding the issues listed in Table 20. The survey was taken before the Letter of John Paul II on Priestly Ordination and other documents that followed, indicating that women cannot be ordained and the issue is not open to discussion. We do not know what effect those pronouncements have had on this topic.

The issues in Table 20 need to be nuanced. The question was not, "Do you favor a certain position on these issues?" but "Do you think Catholics should have a voice in deciding them?" In their pastoral letter on economic justice, the U.S. bishops said that participation in the decisions that affect people's lives (i.e., a share in power) is as much a matter of justice as an equitable share in the world's resources. Our data indicate that the desire of Catholics to participate in decisions that significantly affect their lives is alive and real. The percentile drops below 50 percent only among the Chr communities (on divorce, abortion, and priesthood).

There is no surprise in these statistics. As I have indicated elsewhere, one of the major shifts in Western culture was the end of feudal models and the quest for participative structures in the body politic, as indicated and symbolized in both the French and American Revolutions (Lee, 1996, 70–102). This widespread desire naturally expresses itself on the part of religious people to have a voice in decisions that shape the culture of their institutions.

Table 19
Ideological Self-Identification

Position	GSC			Chr			CTA		
	HS	SC	CO	HS	SC	CO	HS	SC	CO
Religion									
Conserv.	44%	44%	34%	81%	83%	83%	15%	14%	11%
Moderate	23	21	14	14	13	13	15	19	23
Liberal	33	35	52	5	5	4	70	67	66
Politics									
Conserv.	42	44	36	80	85	74	15	13	15
Moderate	24	21	18	16	10	22	15	18	17
Liberal	34	35	46	4	5	4	70	69	68

	ECC			GRC/NG		
	HS	SC	CO	HS	SC	CO
Religion						
Conserv.	5%	4%	7%	37%	44%	46%
Moderate	3	2	2	21	17	13
Liberal	92	94	91	42	39	41
Politics						
Conserv.	7	6	7	41	43	48
Moderate	14	13	11	23	19	19
Liberal	79	81	82	36	38	33

The data in Table 21 clearly affirm the attachment of SCCs to Catholic identity. All three of the largest groups, as well as CTA, are about 15–20 percentage points above the general Catholic population in feeling that there is something special about being Catholic.

Religious Experience

We thought it would be insightful to learn to what extent SCC members claim to have had a personal religious experience (see Table 22). This question was worded: "Have you ever had a religious experience—that is, a particularly powerful religious insight or awakening?"

Table 20
Having a Voice on Issues

Issues	GSC	H/L*	Chr	CTA/ECC		GRC/NG
How parish income is spent	89%	69%	80%	95%	94%	82%
Economic justice, welfare	74	83	63	96	94	78
World peace	69	92	57	94	91	77
Teaching on divorce	53	75	36	78	88	73
Teaching on abortion	51	75	35	75	81	66
Choosing parish priests	53	58	31	87	92	71
Ordaining single women	55	42	21	93	67	67
Ordaining married women	50	22	16	75	90	65

*Asterisk indicates a smaller return on the attitudes survey.

This is a remarkable piece of information. Members of small Christian communities claim to have had a religious experience in notably higher numbers than the general Catholic population that does not belong to any small religious group. Chrs are predictably the highest. Though the smallest of the groups, CTA/ECCs are also high in claiming religious experiences. We do not know, however, anything about the *kinds* of experiences that people claimed to have had.

In *Varieties of Religious Experience*, William James emphasizes the importance of the "force of personal faith" (James, 1958, 101). In language that may seem a bit loaded today, he distinguishes between the chronic religion of the many and the acute religion of the few (Ibid.). In the first case, people are living in a religious tradition created through the religious experience of someone other than themselves, and encoded in the culture of a religious institution, but that has not generated any religious experience for them personally. In the second case, the inherited tradition is usually maintained, but reinforced by an individual's personal religious experience, which perhaps even

Table 21
Attitudes about Being Catholic

Catholicism	GSC	H/L*	Chr	CTA/ECC		GRC/NG
Something special about being Catholic						
agree	77%	75%	81%	75%	44%	62%
don't know, not sure	8	6	4	10	12	8
disagree	11	3	8	14	41	30
Can't imagine being any other religion						
agree	82	75	79	60	47	75
don't know, not sure	4	8	9	10	12	2
disagree	11	0	2	19	35	23

*Asterisk indicates a smaller return on the attitudes survey.

subjected the tradition to some new transformation or reinterpretation. Thus, a new religious experience, usually mediated by the tradition in some way, further empowers it with new energy and insight. The data indicate that SCC members claim to have had religious experience at a higher rate than typical Catholics, an important insight into the kind of religious appetite that motivates SCC membership.

Hazarding a Sociological Comment on SCC Members

In her analysis of religious communities, Patricia Wittberg uses a category from the sociology of religion that is useful in our own examination of SCCs (Wittberg, 1996, 19–31). Most societies or organizations have members with great energy and enthusiasm. In the context of religious groups, the category is that of the religious *virtuoso* (pl. *virtuosi*). As Wittberg notes, the language is a bit unfortunate, for it can conjure up the notion of an elite group. (Even Max Weber, who invented the language, was somewhat uncomfortable with its possible elitist ring.) But that is not what is meant. These are the people who

Table 22
Had a Religious Experience?

	GSC	H/L*	Chr	CTA/ECC		GRC/NG
Yes!	49%	39%	85%	75%	72%	29%

*Asterisk indicates a smaller return on the attitudes survey.

are up for a larger commitment and involvement than the normal life of the community either regularly offers or expects. Llana Silber describes it as "an extreme urge to go beyond everyday life and average norms of achievement" (Wittberg, 1996, 229). Religious virtuosi are important to the vitality of any religious community. SCC members are not the only religious virtuosi in the contemporary Roman Catholic Church. However, they are a significant minority. It is helpful to the church at large to know what it is that engages religious virtuosi in the contemporary world. This information can provide clues to the future development of ecclesial life.

In much of its history, monasteries and religious orders were an important place for religious virtuosi. The ideological interpretation of celibacy as a life of perfection offered a supportive rationale. The position of Vatican II is that all Christians are called to the same perfection and that marriage as well as celibacy is a charism of perfection. This reading removed an important ideological support for celibacy and thus for religious life.

SCC members do more than parish life regularly asks or expects, and more than most Catholics do. They are strongly committed, active Catholics. It may be that SCCs are offering the virtuosi an option that for many women and men replaces religious life.

PART TWO:
WHY PEOPLE BECOME
AND REMAIN SCC MEMBERS

Introduction

For the purposes of understanding SCCs from the inside out, the reasons for joining and the reasons for maintaining membership offer some of the best insights (Table 23).

Table 23
Most Important Personal Reason for Joining

Reasons	GSC	H/L	Chr	CTA/ECC	
Prayer, praise, worship	4%	4%	24%	8%	0%
Community	7	2	12	29	33
Social support, new friends	27	12	21	26	9
Spirituality	17	9	24	14	15
Conversion experience	3	3	15	1	4
New liturgy	0	0	0	13	33
Renew or workshop	5	0	0	0	0
Outreach	3	5	0	2	8
Encouraged by family, friend	8	0	3	8	2
Learn about religion, God	35	61	7	0	3
Meaning of life, problems	0	5	4	0	0
Get closer to God, dedicate life to God	4	10	10	1	0
Alternative to traditional church	4	0	0	12	21
Help marriage, family	0	9	0	0	0
Other	0	0	0	7	2

The highest reason given (61 percent) among H/L members is the desire to learn more about God and religion. This was also relatively high (35 percent) among the GSC members.

Most of those who gave as a reason the need for an alternative church were ECC (21 percent) and CTA (12 percent) members. They are also the only two groups that gave a desire for new liturgy as a reason (33 percent and 13 percent, respectively). We would guess a probable correlation between dissatisfaction with the traditional church and the desire for fresh liturgy.

As a principal reason for joining, the desire for outreach is small. Judging from other data, however, it is clearly not missing from SCC concerns (see Table 24). It just does not turn up for many as the principal reason for joining a community.

While community and relational reasons are certainly not opposed to religious reasons, I thought it would be useful to compare percentages under life experience reasons (community, social support and making new friends, meaning of life and life's problems, and help with marriage and family unity) with explicit God and religion reasons (prayer, praise and worship, spirituality, conversion experience, learning about God and religion, dedicating life to God and getting close to God).

Especially in the three major groups, religious reasons are quite high. But in all groups, relationships rank high—in CTA communities, they rank higher than religious motives for joining.

Having inquired what the principal reason for becoming a member was, in Table 25 we thought it important also to ask: "Once you are a member, what is the best part of being in an SCC?"

This question was framed like the previous one, asking only for *the* best part of SCC life. The quality of relationships is the principal draw. I would certainly guess that we are meeting here the need for community that is a feature of U.S. cultural life, as I indicated in the previous chapter. But it is not merely that.

The fact is, also, that the reasons for there being a community are religious, and it is important not to separate the two. This kind of intimate community where prayer and scripture are part of interpersonal interaction is precisely what cannot happen at the level of parish-wide community, nor is it normally part of the activity of traditional Catholic groups like a holy name society or an altar society.

Having inquired about the best parts of the SCC experience, we also asked SCC members what the most troublesome aspect was (see Table 26).

When asked what community members experienced as most troublesome in the SCC life, they said *nothing* more than any difficulty that was named! The other two categories that help draw the picture are about human relationships/human vulnerability and busy people. In these communities, as in any community, human relationships are sometimes troublesome. Finally, Americans are busy

Table 24
Comparing Reasons for Joining

What kind of reason	GSC	H/L	Chr	CTA/ECC	
Life experience reasons	34%	27%	37%	55%	42%
God and religion reasons	63	87	80	24	56

Table 25
Best Part of SCC Participation

Best Part	GSC	H/L	Chr	CTA/ECC	
*Sharing, exchanging	27%	12%	12%	29%	22%
Personal or spiritual growth	13	27	18	12	16
*Community, friendship	51	30	28	35	46
Learning	15	16	2	1	0
Prayer, praise, worship	4	4	19	8	0
Gifts of the Holy Spirit	0	0	9	4	4
Outreach	3	6	6	4	6
Relationship with God	4	10	18	4	12
Freedom from institutional church	0	0	0	18	26
Improves marriage, family life	0	3	0	0	0
Other	0	5	3	4	0
*Quality of Relationships: combining "Sharing, exchanging" and "Community, friendship"	78	42	40	64	68

Table 26
Most Troublesome Aspect

	GSC	H/L	Chr	CTA/ECC	
Time, scheduling demands	29%	4%	22%	23%	13%
*Disagreement, dominating personalities	10	2	9	7	21
*Difficulty in sharing	11	9	2	5	4
*Exposes human weakness	3	0	3	2	1
Absenteeism of members	11	2	21	5	16
Challenges to faith	4	0	2	0	5
Church interference, rejection	1	0	5	7	10
Nothing	30	57	15	27	10
Other	1	26	21	24	20
*Combined relational issues	24	11	14	14	26

people, especially families that must address children's needs and activities. So they have said that finding time and making a workable schedule are not always easy. The different reasons assembled in *other* are too diverse to draw any kind of a picture.

Summary

There are minimally 37,000 small Christian communities in the U.S. Catholic Church, in all regions of the country, with a membership (adults and children) of between 750,000 and 1,000,000. On the average, SCCs have 13–17 adult members. Our largest group of SCCs, about 24,000 communities (65% percent of the total), are mostly connected with parish life, and with some frequency have a relationship with national SCC organizations. We have called them the general type small community. Hispanic/Latino communities, whose membership is virtually all Hispanic/Latino, are about 7,550 strong (20 percent of the total). The level of education and income in these communities is lower than in any of the others. There are about 4,800 charismatic communities (12 percent of the total). Members are the most traditional in beliefs and church allegiance. Call to Action communities and Eucharist Centered Communities are each less than 100 in number (less than 1 percent of the total). These are the best educated Catholics with the highest income. They are the most solidly committed to social justice and the most independent in their relationship to church and church issues.

Most community members are middle-aged and above (40+)—over 75 percent in three of the groups, including the largest of the GSCs. We should be deeply concerned about the paucity of young adult members (only 18 percent among GSCs, the largest group). SCC membership is slightly more affluent and considerably better educated than the general Catholic population (except for H/L communities).

Much new activity suggests that the movement itself is growing. Among GSCs, 44 percent are three years old or less. The groups with the greatest longevity are Chrs and ECCs, with 54 percent and 45 percent, respectively, of communities that are eleven years old or older. These two groups also have the lowest percentage of new groups.

SCC members identify prayer and family issues as their highest values. Spiritual matters and helping others are also important. Most members pray daily or pray often—GSCs 92 percent; H/Ls 75 percent; Chrs 94 percent—in comparison with the general population at 66 percent. Over 80 percent overall say that their SCC experience is deeply satisfying, which is not surprising since the values they named (prayer and spiritual matters) get high marks in SCC life. In all groups, members name personal contacts as the greatest influence on their own interest in SCCs (which should be a clue to the recruitment of new members).

Weekly participation in Eucharist is the case for upward of 90 percent for the three largest groups of SCCs (97 percent of the total), which compares with 32 percent for the general Catholic population. Among these same three groups, about 85 percent are parish connected, although three-fourths of communities meet in members' homes, not in church buildings. There are considerably more SCC members who say they have had a religious experience (GSC 49 percent, H/L 39 percent, Chr 85 percent, CTA 75 percent, ECC 72 percent) than in the general Catholic population (29 percent). SCC members are also far more likely to be eucharistic ministers, lectors, or ushers than the general Catholic population. They are also less likely to consider ever leaving the church than the general Catholic population. In a word, SCC members are church-going, praying people, connected with church and loyal.

SCC members do not differ much with the general Catholic population in identifying themselves as conservative, moderate, or liberal in both church and civil matters. Increased education tends to put more members on the liberal side. Like all U.S. Catholics, SCC members feel the tension between loyalty to the pope/church and their own conscience/experience, increasingly so with more education. They expect formal authority to make its case with reasons. Also, like most Catholics (a little more so), SCC members believe they should have a say in most areas of church practice and thought. And more strongly than the general Catholic population, SCC members believe that there is indeed something special about being Catholic (GSC 87 percent, H/L 75 percent, Chr 81 percent).

When asked why they became members of SCCs, both religious reasons (e.g., spirituality, to learn about God) and relational reasons (social support, community) rank high (for GSCs, God and religion at 63 percent, relational reasons at 34 percent). However, when asked what is the best part of being an SCC member, the relational/community reasons grow in importance. Asked to name the most problematic aspect of SCC life, more said *nothing* than any other answer. The next highest has to do with time and scheduling. The relative lack of any large problematic issues corresponds to the high degree of satisfaction that SCC members experience in their small Christian communities.

SCCs seem to be meeting both religious and relational needs that are not met in traditional parish life. But they do not pull people away from parish life because members are strongly connected with institutional church life.

4

What SCCs Do When They Gather and What Difference It Makes
Creating Communities, Forming Selves, Touching the World, Engaging the Catholic Heritage and Human Experience

The following account is from a member of a largely professional group that meets every two weeks to address scripture, asking: "How does this good news shape our presence in the dynamic life of this city?" They meet at 7:30 A.M. every other Monday. Most are active in their respective parishes. The description is cited at length because it names so many of the pieces of life and relationships in small Christian communities.

> Recently I have been involved in a group that came together to reflect on the gospels. There's an interesting mix of occupations and professions, a rare blend of generations, too. Some are in their twenties, others in their late forties, some even in their sixties. There are lawyers, journalists, writers, academics in a variety of fields. Hardly anyone has been preoccupied with "insider" or churchy issues. Instead, our faith-commitment has seemed to point us outward: toward the city, the political order, questions of how to live.
>
> We meet every other week, early in the morning. By mutual agreement we've read some part of scripture. Doggedly we've moved through Mark, Matthew, Luke, Acts. We've used

commentaries to try to "get at" the meaning more readily, or to help reconstruct the scene in our imaginations. One of the group signs on to prepare and lead the rest. There's no set order of prayer, though we do generally begin and end by praying.

What often happens is that when I least expect it, Jesus is present—not mystically, but vividly—because of someone's quick reaction, because of another person's crabby resistance to the text, because we have worked at bringing his times closer to ours. In a recent session (we are using Andrew Overman's *Church and Community in Crisis* to guide us through Matthew) we imagined Jesus calling the fishermen to drop their nets. Then we imagined them heading around Galilee, hanging out in synagogues (gathering places). Overman helped us to recreate the scene freshly again. "Given the relatively small size of Lower Galilee and close proximity of the Galilean places…there is no need to assume that those who supposedly followed Jesus never came home again…. A more likely scenario is the group gathered around Jesus, being out on the road for a day or two, and then returning to their homes and town…. One could easily travel with Jesus for several days, or even one day, get to a Galilean town, engage in an argument with local leaders, and be home by nightfall." Suddenly the whole gospel situation made sense to us. It was not so very different from our situation. We were also gathering, hanging out, wanting to be friends with Jesus, wanting to learn from him.

Another time we were doing the early chapters of Matthew. Somehow we got onto the question of how the community of Matthew retrieved and processed its memories of Jesus and how those (presumably diverse) stories and snatches were smoothed out into a coherent narrative.

Near the end of that discussion, one of our group, a journalist, launched out into a comparison between our group's way of telling stories and that of Matthew's community. "At some point," he said, "they took all the bits and pieces and handed them over to someone in the group who could write…and said, 'Okay, here, you write this down.' Was that the way it was?" One of our group is a scholar with a strong grasp of what the early centuries could have been like. "Probably something pretty much like that," he said.

Then, laughter. What was so funny? Well, nothing was precisely funny, but I notice that almost every really good insight in the group fosters a sudden expression of delight. So one of the main characteristics of our group is laughter.

Later, when I began to reflect on all this, I noticed something else: the way the insight blooms. Often, at the beginning, there are awkward pockets of silence. The text baffles us. People feel stuck. Then as one comment is stacked on another, a major connection is made. The infancy narratives led us into a discussion of the ways power is exercised in society. We manage to make connections between the leadership of Moses and Jesus. Everything comes alive as some long-glossed-over part of the story begins to yield contemporary meanings.

Part of the joy is in the worldliness of the group. People bring real-world knowledge to their gospel reflections. Each one looks through the lens of his or her own life: a lawyer; a teacher; a graduate student; a cradle Catholic or a convert; one with a particular focus on justice questions; one who cares especially about city life.

A recent discussion was about the way power is exercised, not through the legal system, but outside of it, through individual power brokers who influence the way things get done and what gets done. The pressures bearing down on the community of Matthew seem to be our pressures, too. We wrestle with the Beatitudes, trying to make them ours, fresh and cutting-edge as we know they should be.

I was not prepared, fully, for the warm affection that has sprung up among us. In so short a time! Friendships have sprouted; we look forward to these sessions, and to the occasional evening socials, where the meaning of table fellowship is clear.

I like this group. These people are church for me. They help me to see Jesus freshly and to hear his teachings spoken clearly again.

We are all storytellers, I think. And the gospel itself (being the master story) calls us (insistently, continually, disconcertingly) into new ways of conversion. Reluctantly (without even meaning to) we listen; we respond; we cough up stories from the distant past, moments of insight, hopes for the future. Others, sitting on the other side of the room, fiddling with the ribbons on their Bibles, or staring at a funny place in the carpet, hear some curious observation, something that connects. "I know what you mean about that." "I used to have a friend who...."

"When we lived in California...." "When the children were younger...." "We had a pastor once who used to say...."

From a thousand directions it comes: reflection on the Word. A certain wisdom bubbles up from the text, from our willingness to read and be guided by it, from our attentiveness, from our friendship. We are not so churchy as to call ourselves disciples. Maybe the language embarrasses us. Maybe "ministry" sounds too formal; still we are gathered in faith, willing to be led by the text and changed by the story.

When we want to follow Jesus in our late twentieth-century lives, the ways to lead and follow are not always so obvious. Through telling our own stories; the stories of our organizations; through reflecting on the bits and pieces of the Jesus story, on narratives of community here and there, through the discipline of study, of fixing our eyes on the text and circling around in the margins, suddenly we get it.

Leadership is formed this way. When we forget what genuine leadership looks like, Jesus of Nazareth reminds us. He offers no theory of leadership. His teachings are not so novel; his sayings are not so hard to grasp; but the quality of his leadership is so blindingly self-evident we just plain want to do that, too.

PART ONE:
WHAT COMMUNITIES DO WHEN THEY GATHER

Introduction

Whatever their motivations for joining an SCC, between 750,000 and 1,000,000 Catholics meet regularly in such groups, most weekly. What do these Catholics do when they gather? What do their activities mean for their lives, for the Catholic Church in the United States, and for the larger society? When Catholics gather in their SCCs they participate in community and engage their Catholic heritage, including scripture, as they think about and address the challenges of their daily lives. Whether they reflect on it consciously or not, they also are reconstructing their relationships to their Catholic Christian heritage and their Roman Catholic denomination. Finally, they are negotiating a way to remain

Catholic in the pluralistic and highly individualistic social and cultural context of the United States.

All of these things happen in a series of activities that occur in SCCs when Catholics constitute themselves in a community after they gather and greet one another. The SCC meeting time is both part of the routine of members' lives and, for most, a special time that modifies and revises the meaning of all the rest of their lives.

Members express the significance of this act of gathering when they talk about the meaning of their SCCs for them: "They're just like an extended family, you know. We know their lives. They know our lives. We evolved together" (GSC). "We don't have family here. Our SCC is our family" (H/L). "You can see sometimes in the others, more than ourselves, the way God is touching and leading and growing. It makes a difference in the group as a whole, and it also makes a difference in you, but there is this awareness that somehow we are being touched and enabled to grow through our coming together" (GSC). "It's not just me and God. God is important for me in a personal way, but works through the community" (Chr).

Community becomes tangible for members in their groups; it moves from "theoretical" to "experiential" (GSC). The SCC is a place of face-to-face encounters within a group of small enough scale that members can know one another well: "…I love the intimacy and the sharing and what can happen in the small group" (Chr).

SCCs are a context for community, support, and transformation. What happens to members in their groups meets the needs and longings that brought them to an SCC, and sometimes transforms people's needs and longings. As one person put it, "But in general, we are meeting together here, we have get-togethers in our homes, to share different things, play, to get to know one another, sometimes on retreats, sometimes in the community. But the truth is that this is primordial, this is life, really" (H/L).

Those are strong statements and claims about the role and power of small Christian communities in the lives of hundreds of thousands of contemporary Roman Catholics in the United States. What are these people doing, then, that means so much to them? Here is what communities say about their gatherings, their activities, and some of the dynamics of their group life.

Table 27
Frequency of Meetings

How often?	GSC	H/L	Chr	CTA/ECC	
Weekly	35%	81%	79%	15%	57%
Biweekly	37	15	11	48	20
Every 3 weeks	2	—	1	2	—
Monthly	17	3	4	29	16
Other	10	—	2	5	7

Frequency of Gatherings

It is remarkable that most groups meet weekly or biweekly, 90 percent for H/L and Chr communities (Table 27). It is our judgment, both from the quantitative data and the interviews, that SCCs are a major context for members' faith lives. That should be clear from the discussion above. They are not just one more committee meeting. Being a significant context for life is best served by weekly or biweekly meetings that facilitate felt continuity. Active memory of last week and anticipation of next week function easily in a one- or two-week span. The cohesiveness of community is served well by this frequency.

Where Communities Gather

The numbers sometimes exceed 100 percent because some groups meet in more than one place (see Table 28). Several things deserve attention. The first is that a large majority of the two largest groups, GSCs and H/Ls, meet in members' homes, and that is true also of the CTA groups. This may mark a new ecclesial instinct in the making. Roman Catholics have long felt that home is a holy place. They have had new homes blessed and kept holy pictures and crucifixes in visible places. And, of course, they knew themselves to be church members. But only in recent decades is there a retrieval from the experience of the early centuries that people are doing something in their homes that is a church experience: Home is where something called church sometimes also happens.

Elsewhere, Michael Cowan and I have reflected upon differ-ent ways that SCCs fence with the churchhood issue (Cowan/Lee,

Table 28
Meeting Place

Place	GSC	H/L	Chr	CTA/ECC	
Member's Home	76%	93%	26%	78%	50%
Public Bldg	3	2	1	2	7
Parish Bldg	30	16	70	15	10
Other	6	5	15	14	49

1997, 36–61). Descriptively, whenever church is being lived, at least these four traits are discernible: *koinonia*, or community—people participating in each other's lives; *diakonia*, or service, within and beyond the group; *kerygma*, the centrality of the good news of Jesus Christ; and *leitourgia*, or liturgy, forms of prayer common to the ecclesial community (often Liturgy of the Word). These are not prescriptive, that is, one cannot just do them and say, "We are church." But descriptively, when they are happening, something akin to churchhood is afoot. And these are precisely happening in homes. This looks like an important contemporary development. For SCCs, churchhood tends to be an interesting question and an important one, but not a tortured issue.

The Main Practices of Small Christian Communities

This is clearly some of the most significant data, for they tell us what communities are doing that engages their hearts and their minds (Table 29). Though communities certainly do not all do exactly the same thing, clearly discernible patterns exist.

Before commenting on the data, I would like to remark on several items. I am not sure about the readings on weekend Eucharist and home Eucharist. From interviews and from other data, for example, I think it very unlikely that 34 percent of H/Ls have weekend Eucharist as a regular part of their gathering. I suspect some answered that they as individuals participated in a weekend Eucharist (probably in the parish, since such a high percentage of them are parish connected). Observations and interviews revealed that ECCs celebrated weekend Eucharist in several settings, including members' homes.

Table 29
The Activities/Practices at Every Meeting

Activities	GSC	H/L	Chr	CTA/ECC	
Prayer	92%	97%	100%	92%	80%
Faith sharing	83	78	85	83	59
Read, discuss scripture	78	94	76	70	63
Spirituality	58	61	75	61	59
Group silence	30	32	64	38	30
Weekend Eucharist	0	34	25	15	64
Theological reflection	24	22	12	32	33
Sharing visions	20	18	21	32	31
Evangelization	3	45	30	3	3
Home Eucharist	3	4	6	4	34

Also, I am not sure that *theological reflection* was understood in the way the question was intended. It was not about reading or discussing theology. We meant to ask whether members reflected on experience in the light of their faith. It is clear from interviews and transcriptions of meetings that in almost all gatherings this takes place, but not under the rubric of theological reflection.

I will focus first on the four major activities in which SCCs engage most. Then I will devote attention to an area where our theological team believes there is room to grow (and where it is important to grow).

Prayer, Faith Sharing, Scripture, and Spirituality

When SCC members gather weekly or biweekly their four most regular activities across all types of groups are:

(1) Prayer (GSC 92 percent, H/L 97 percent, Chr 100 percent, and 86 percent CTA/ECC 86 percent).

(2) Faith sharing (GSC 85 percent, H/L 78 percent, Chr 85 percent, CTA/ECC 71 percent).

(3) Scripture (GSC 78 percent, 94 percent, H/L 94 percent, Chr 76 percent, CTA/ECC 66 percent).

(4) Spirituality (GSC 58 percent, H/L 61 percent, Chr 75 percent, CTA/ECC 60 percent).

While each category of SCC engages in these activities in its own distinctive way, their commonalities are more striking than their differences. Less frequently, SCCs share visions, have home Eucharist, and engage in activities that they identify as *evangelization*. In one instance, however, evangelization is practiced at every meeting by 45 percent of the H/Ls. For H/Ls, evangelization has some of the capacity of what other types of SCCs describe as faith sharing. (It may be that the language of evangelization is more familiar in Catholic H/L culture than in other groups.)

We did not ask participants to apportion the amount of time spent on each activity in an SCC meeting. Interviews and observations during later stages of our research, as well as comments from leaders who filled out the census questionnaire, show that the four main activities blend into each other in the life of groups as do some of the lesser identified activities. It still is possible, however, to describe something of their focus and rhythm.

All of these things happen in a series of activities that occur in SCCs when Catholics constitute themselves in a community after they gather and greet one another. Creating and being part of a community are central to SCC members, whether the SCC is small like many of the GSCs (8–13 members) or large like some Chrs and CTA/ECCs (50–70 members). In and through that tangible experience of community participants find themselves changed in many ways. For the first time, one person was able "to kneel, and to look honestly into our God's eyes" (GSC). Another described how "listening to the personal stories and testimonies of many other people, I have a deeper sense of a personal relationship with God, and the importance of the community being open to God. And I have a sense of this being a small community as a part of a much bigger community…" (Chr). Another described her SCC as the place where she came to "know that [God] cares about me" (Chr).

Interviews indicate that for some the SCC is the first place where they have felt free to speak or have become aware that they have something to say. In H/L communities some learn to read motivated by the desire to read the Word of God. Others find themselves able to speak out, to be less judgmental, to be more patient with family members, and to appreciate qualities in others they had not seen before.

Many SCC members find themselves propelled from their group into more active involvement in their parishes and, for some, in their worlds. As one person put it: "Through being at the prayer meeting and God touching my heart, I got to the point where I'm at today, to let them [residents at the Rescue Mission] touch you and you touch them back. There is something beyond the smell and deeper than the cleanliness" (Chr). Involvement in SCCs creates an awareness of problems in neighborhoods and personal and corporate responsibility to address them. It also leads participants to begin to reflect on how contemporary life lacks structures that existed for people in earlier times—extended families, neighborhoods, and so forth. All of these statements are supported by interviews and/or the observations of SCC members.

The transformations that occur in the lives of SCC members do not happen simply because a group gathers. SCCs come together in faith, in the name of Jesus. People arrive desiring, if not always believing, that something will happen that might bring them closer to God, help them to live more faithfully. Some come to realize that "our spirituality is our living" (Chr).

A combination of the community experience in the name of Jesus and the activities that are constitutive of that experience creates a context where SCC members find themselves changed in many ways in relation to themselves, their families, their world, and their church. To understand how this happens, we will focus individually on the four main activities.

1. Prayer

"Having people who can pray with me" was one of the reasons people gave for seeking out an SCC. In some groups participants take turns preparing rituals related to the liturgical year, scripture study for the day, or life events of members of the group. In some groups arranging prayer is the responsibility of the leader. Other SCCs rely on prayers that are included with the materials they use for discussing scripture. Still others, notably Chrs, value spontaneous prayer. The use of hymns or psalms in prayer varies across groups.

Prayer in SCCs is addressed directly to God, Jesus, or the Spirit, and draws on the images, symbols, and texts of the Catholic tradition and on members' experiences of God. Prayer in SCCs seems to draw little, however, on the contemplative or meditative prayer traditions in Catholicism. Prayer unites the group into a community, enacts participants' bonds to their Catholic heritage, and for many legitimates their SCC as a Catholic and/or religious activity.

SCC prayer is primarily verbal. Only charismatic SCCs practice group silence weekly in any significant degree (Table 29). SCCs pray about their lives, their communities, and the world. Their prayer is intensely and intentionally incarnational. "We pray for one another, pray for our children, pray for our neighbors, pray for healing" (GSC).

This style of prayer brings people to God and changes the way participants think about God's presence: "...I used to think that God was sort of removed and now I know that God is present in each of us, you know, in a way that I never would have understood prior to now" (GSC). "Jesus Christ has become much more real to me because of my small community involvement" (GSC). "I think I'm more aware of what's going on in the world. I'm more cognizant and want to learn more" (GSC). One understood better what it means to "be a steward with the gift of the natural world" (GSC). Another grappled with seeing Christ in those we ignore (GSC). Prayer in SCCs seems to dispose members to enter reflectively and more deeply into their lives and worlds and to seek God's presence there. Some SCC members find themselves praying more because of their SCC involvement (H/L).

CTA/ECC groups speak less directly of prayer in the interview and observation data, but more about ministry, justice, and finding a community that keeps them connected to the church.

2. Faith Sharing

Faith sharing is a weekly activity in 80 percent or more of GSCs, H/Ls, Chrs, and CTAs. ECCs also include it weekly but less than the other types, probably because they participate in Eucharist at every session more than any other type, and do not identify Eucharist specifically as faith sharing.

For many people in GSCs, the SCC experience is where they realize that God is with them, an insight that comes to them often through the experience of sharing their lives and faith with others. "If you realize all the circumstances, you know what a godsend a small Christian community was to me" (GSC). This is a widely shared perception whether the group stands by a woman whose husband is dying of cancer, or a person going through a divorce, job loss, and more (GSC; H/L).

Faith sharing in GSCs focuses on members telling each other how God is working in their lives, where they are looking for God in their lives, and their efforts to discern faithful actions in their family lives, work, and communities. This understanding is congruent with what GSC participants would have experienced in RENEW groups.

The SCC is a place where members, without embarrassment, can discuss their effort to be faithful. One CTA group described itself as "starving [for] this type of connection." Participants wanted "somebody to open the Word with and to share" (CTA).

Faith sharing directs attention to the experience of individuals in the group. By this focus, it locates religious reality and increases the capacity of an individual's experience in the equation of religious authority. Faith sharing in SCCs creates a space within which religious realities that transcend everyday life can be taken seriously and related to everyday life.

The SCC is a place where members can bring all dimensions of their lives: "I think being a part of the small community has helped me integrate the whole person, the whole, you know, into a spiritual sense much more, because, you are more involved in prayer and scripture and everything all kind of rolled into one. It is really hard to tell where one leaves, stops, and the next one starts. It becomes a much more natural part of life" (GSC). The SCC makes faith "just a part of the fibre of one's life" (GSC).

Catholic laity in groups want God to be real for them. That desire is expressed in Chrs, which of all the types have had the most groups in existence for the longest time. The experience of the Holy Spirit validates God's reality in their lives. In ECCs, the reality of God is focused in the communal celebration of the Eucharist in a meaningful manner. GSC members are more likely to be searching for God in their lives.

Much of faith sharing connects with what we would consider theological reflection: understanding our lives in the light of faith and having our lives enriched by those insights. If people do not have regular time with a group that is known and trusted, this kind of sharing—this way of creating meaning by which to live—is far less likely to occur.

3. Reading and Discussion of Scripture

Reading and discussion of scripture is the third most common activity in SCCs. Particularly in GSCs, the primary focus is on members' lives and on scripture. Participants are engaged in a conversation, sometimes self-consciously and sometimes not, between their lived experience, including their larger world, and the scriptures. The GSCs' focus on life experience and scripture shows that developing in these groups is an understanding and experience of church that, while it has antecedents in several periods of the church's past, seems unfamiliar to those who experienced the abundance of priests and religious that made the devotional, eucharistically centered Catholicism of the first two-thirds of the twentieth century in the United States possible. SCCs resonate with Vatican Council II's reappropriation of scripture as central to Catholic life.

Most members of GSCs are eager to study and discuss scripture; they want to "become knowledgeable about it" (GSC). Most participants in these groups grew up in a church that did not emphasize scripture. Some feel their SCC gives them access to God's Word that was kept from them early in their Catholic experience. A woman in her seventies talked about how she had not read the Bible because she could not comprehend it, but when she joined the group she began to read *and* understand it. "But I think it would have been nice if we as Catholics could have got more into the Bible when we were really young" (GSC). Another described the ability "to quote scripture" as a "wonderful experience" (GSC).

The encounter with scripture is particularly precious to members of H/L SCCs. "And [in those days]…the Catholic Church didn't open the Bible…. Not with a lot of desire, but it [did begin to] open the Bible. And then there, we found a Christ who loves us, who tells us go, and love. As I have loved you" (H/L). Many distinguish between "having their faith out of the gospel" and out of "many traditions" of the old church. "And now, more the Word, try to live it, and share it" (H/L).

Readings for the coming Sunday often are the focus of scripture discussions. Members wait to see if what they talked about in their group will be in the homily in any way. Sharing and discussing the readings takes groups back to their lives and world as well. One participant summed up well the result of this in reference to his experience working in a soup kitchen: "...one of them [the beggars, poor, old, disadvantaged in the food line] is actually in the form of Christ. So that I have to look for, and look at, each one of them as a part of God and a part of Christ that's standing in that line" (GSC). One SCC member observed: "The scriptures come alive to us now rather than as just words on a page" (Chr).

The two most widely used resources for reading and discussing scripture are *Quest*, developed by the Office for Small Communities from the Hartford Diocese, and *Sunday by Sunday*, published by the Sisters of St. Joseph of Carondelet in St. Paul, Minnesota. The two programs are lectionary-based. Each presents central themes or issues in scripture for Sunday with reflections and questions designed to help adults identify with the heart of the biblical passages and to see where these touch their own lives. The *Quest* material is more didactic in approach, more oriented toward exegesis and then application of the scripture lessons. It provides songs and an order for prayer that many groups use. *Sunday by Sunday*, more than *Quest*, tends to focus on key images in the scripture readings, and to use questions to help adults identify both affectively and cognitively with the scripture meanings. It does not emphasize steps for action as strongly each week as does *Quest*.

Both *Quest* and *Sunday by Sunday* are effective resources for helping SCC groups to bring members' lives into conversation with their Catholic Christian heritage in scripture. The regular practice of engaging scripture and asking what it means in terms of members' lives creates a context for insight into both. "But I know that many of them are learning about the Word of God and a relationship with

Jesus. And how it affects their lives everyday and dealing with Mom and Dad, or going to school or working" (GSC).

How the insight comes and how the connection is made between members' lives and the scriptural and theological heritage of Catholicism are not something about which SCC members or leaders seem to be methodologically self-conscious. When asked in interviews if they could retrieve experiences in their groups when they "had an unexpected insight that has altered the way you see life or see the group," some members tried to express the serendipity and graced nature of the experience.

One respondent referred to a woman as "someone with insight" because she knew exactly what to say when others attacked the Catholic Church in her presence. Another respondent tried to express insight with a fuller example: once, when driving down the street, he could not even look at a young woman who was asking for money. "But, what bothered me beyond that [his belief that giving money to people on the street isn't a good thing to do] was that I couldn't even look her in the eye; I just wanted to avoid her completely as if she didn't exist. And how bad that made me feel and then this scripture really brought it all back and I said, 'Oh my God I really did do something bad there.' To not even be able to relate to a person on that small level, to be able to look them in the eye and smile at them, you know. That's pretty sad. So, yeah, and I think that if you, if people allow it to happen, if we allow it to happen, every single scripture that we work with in the small community you can't help but bring out that side of it, you know, and it has to talk to you on that level. If you allow, it's real easy to glaze over it and kind of ignore it. You can't let that happen" (GSC). Others mentioned discussions of the bishops' draft pastoral on women and the Gulf War. One person described "a movement through the years to more justice in our community" (GSC). Another described the process as moving among events in individuals' lives, the world, and scripture (CTA). This is a solid and brief description of what often occurs in SCC gatherings.

The interview question designed to get directly at how SCCs bring faith and life together was: "What's the process like in your community that brings faith and your own lived experience together in some kind of interaction?" (This was our way of asking whether and/or how theological reflection connected scripture and faith with concrete lived experience.)

One respondent talked about how the use of a medical-ethics text more than discussing the Sunday readings brought faith and life together for that group, mainly because someone in the group was dealing with whatever the subject of the chapter for the week was. "I think this probably was the deepest sharing and the deepest [experience] of bringing into our own family life and what's happening with our kind and whatever, than any resource has ever done. Um, I think it was almost a little scary too, because it was so real" (GSC). Another SCC leader interviewed said this: "I think a lot of this happens in our prayer life together—as we pray for one another…. But I also think, too, that sharing depends on what's in hearts and our minds and what we come with. So it's not like it's divorced; it really is together. People have learned through the years, I think, to put that together." The person continued that when discussing the readings for Sunday "it elicits something you know. And it might be from the newspaper; it might be bigger issues that are going on" (GSC). Another group talked about how they would pray, read scripture, and then things would happen in their lives that they could identify with in the scriptures. This group also noted that they used stories of saints and devotion to Mary in their reflections (GSC). In the interviews and observations with H/L groups answers to questions, like many in the GSCs, had to do concretely with what God has done in their lives. Chr members answered questions much like GSC members: "There is not a day that goes by that I don't take what I've learned there, like the love of God, out into the community" (Chr).

The interview and observation data give little evidence of a sustained critical approach to scripture on the part of SCC group members or leaders, but they provide considerable evidence for exposure to the images and stories from scripture. This, in turn, forms imagination and sparks thinking about SCC members' lives and worlds.

People come to GSCs because they are looking for a deeper, more complex way to articulate and interpret the religious meaning of their lives. They need a scriptural and theological discourse congruent with what they use professionally. The current practice of scripture study in GSCs evidenced in the participant observations is not equal to the desire. This may help to explain the lower satisfaction level of participants in GSCs when compared to participants in ECCs, CTAs, H/Ls, and Chrs (though the motivation survey indicates that the satisfaction level of GSCs is very high).

Evidence occurs repeatedly in interviews and observation data that suggests a growing complexity of thought and perception on the part of SCC members. One Chr participant put it this way: "My own sense of the complexity and the wholeness of the human being, and both our relationship to God, and our community support and love for each other, has expanded immensely." An indication of a growing cognitive complexity on the part of SCC members, one that changes how they think about themselves, their church, and their world, comes through in statements about greater involvement in ministry and more compassion for bishops.

4. Spirituality

The fourth most frequent activity in SCCs was identified on the census as spirituality. The interviews and observations show no direct discussion of spirituality as a distinct topic in GSCs. H/L and Chr group material alludes to talks and presentations that *may* be about topics in spirituality. Nor did the data reveal any instance of the practice of a particular spiritual discipline, such as a new form of prayer or asceticism. A tentative conclusion is that respondents to the census saw spirituality as the category that captured the intention and tone of all the activities in the groups.

Prayer, faith sharing, reading and discussing scripture, and spirituality then are the four main activities that take place in SCCs. They are part of what constitutes the SCC as a community in the name of Jesus. As such, they also are ways that participants in SCCs reconstruct their relationship to their Catholic Christian heritage and denomination.

Social Commitment: Room to Grow

When people were asked to name what is very important to them, prayer and family were first. But over 80 percent in every SCC

Table 30
Social Outreach

Kind of Outreach	GSC	H/L	Chr	CTA/ECC	
Helping each other within the group	23%	31%	17%	19%	27%
Helping others outside the group	16	21	12	18	27
Addressing social issues	8	19	2	25	21

group listed *helping others.* More than half said that *environment* matters. And about a fourth said that *political issues* are very important.

When asked in what issues they would want to have a voice, well over 80 percent named economic justice and welfare policies; almost as many named world peace.

However, Table 30 shows the results of the responses when people were queried as to what their communities do at every meeting in regard to social concerns.

Both the survey data and the observations and interviews reveal that *gathering* is the most rewarding part of SCC experience, and that *being sent,* that is, social outreach, is a problematic dimension of the ecclesial reality of SCCs. And when being sent is operative, far more members understand that as the individual members of the community being sent, not the community as an entity. Some, in fact, reject the notion that being sent should be embodied by the group as a whole.

SCC membership does frequently raise social awareness, but falls short of social action. One member (GSC) said that the community "certainly helped how I see outreach in Matthew 25, and different people." One community leader commented how her group was "struggling together...more and more...to encounter the social gospel" (GSC). Another member remarked that through her community she had learned that "there's a lot more to life than working and amassing a fortune and retiring with all the money you need to come and go as you please," and that as a result "consumerism and the mad rush for consumerism have become a big nonvalue for me" (GSC). A few spoke about being "more aware of what's going on in the world. Being more cognizant and wanting to learn more" (GSC).

Some members were clear that their SCC membership helped them in their professional lives, for example, "to make good business decisions and have good relationships with coworkers" (GSC). But public issues sometimes caused consternation. One member commented on the uneasiness that developed when an attempt was made to discuss the Gulf War: "You could just see the splits, you know, in the group. We had some heated discussions on that" (GSC). When the same group also tried to discuss HIV issues and the death penalty, some members would absent themselves. Another guessed that community members probably did not know much about the church's social teaching. "I don't think for most people that even though you share this faith tradition, at least a sacramental tradition, that they understand the social teaching of the Catholic Church. They haven't been exposed to it. But it's wonderful and it's there" (GSC). In the following comment an interviewee clearly stated feelings of ambiguity:

> Another big thing that we've dealt with is this whole *sent and gathered* thing. Some of the people feel that being gathered is perfectly fine. Others of us feel a very strong need for the sent part of it. Some people say, "But we each do our thing individually, and that's fine. We don't have to do it as a group." And I agree that it is fine; however, I'm not really sure that that's really true in a lot of cases…and if that is true that people individually are doing their own thing, then I would like to have a particular time for everybody to talk about what they are doing, because I think we could really learn a lot from each other (GSC).

When SCCs are considered within their U.S. context, the lack of consciousness and commitment around structural and social justice issues should not be surprising. At no time in the history of the Catholic Church in the United States has extensive knowledge of or loyalty to its social teachings been widespread among its membership. Catholics in the United States live in a society and culture within which political and economic positions are generally understood to be the responsibility of an individual's conscience. They

Table 31
Leadership Patterns by Gender

Gender	GSC	H/L	Chr	CTA/ECC	
Female	54%	71%	40%	53%	33%
Male	24	19	35	26	32
Both	22	10	22	21	35

live in a society in which the discourse of individuals and communities is couched overwhelmingly in terms of individual rights, needs, and satisfactions. To move SCC Catholics to a level of knowledge of and commitment to social teaching would require a long term commitment and skillful leadership. That leadership, if it is to move people, would need to have as its goal helping groups to develop a far more methodologically self-aware and deliberately disciplined process of theological reflection and social analysis.

We think that SCCs are places where the church *could* develop in these directions. But it would take a concerted effort that, while not systematically underway, has networks and the production of materials that *could* be at the disposal of this formation of conscience and social commitment. This would also require far stronger leadership than currently seems to be the case.

Leadership in SCCs

We will first look at gender distribution among leaders, and then examine how leadership is selected and how it appears to function (see Table 31). We will then reflect upon the data.

Only in the very small grouping of ECCs is leadership evenly divided between men and women. In the H/L communities, the large majority of leaders are women (and in Hispanic Catholic life, church attendance generally is considerably higher for women than men). In the largest group, GSCs also show a heavy preponderance of women leaders. As additional context, it is useful to recall from the parish study of the National Pastoral Life Center that of the 29,000-plus nonordained people serving in professional ministry (not including schoolteachers), over 80 percent are women. I would highlight the fact that while women are excluded from official church community leadership as ordained members, in SCCs they lead communities in their relational life, their prayer life, and their public life.

Leadership Designation

All groups must address four developmental issues: those around *belonging* (who belongs and how people become group members); *power issues* (how decisions are made and how accountability functions); *closeness or intimacy issues* (what kinds of closeness and disclosure are appropriate for a particular group at a particular stage of its life); and *effectiveness* (achieving the objectives of the group). Power issues are the most difficult to negotiate clearly and directly. No group can successfully negotiate closeness issues and become effective in its objectives if the power issues have not been addressed. Leadership is not the only power issue, but it is a key one.

SCCs report few *formal structures* of leadership, that is, explicitly established patterns, continuing over time, to guide the exercise of initiative and influence in the group. We will first examine patterns that are reported in the research, and then discuss some of the broader issues of SCC leadership.

At the time of the survey, about half of the GSCs and CTAs had been in existence three years or less (see Table 32). Over 70 percent in both groups reported volunteer leadership or no defined leadership structure (71 percent of GSCs and 78 percent of CTAs). However, between a third and a half (48% percent of GSC and 35 percent of CTAs) maintain some form of parish contact, perhaps indicating some leadership influence from this larger institutional setting: "Individually we see ourselves as connected to parish, but I'm not sure we see ourselves as community connected in that way...there doesn't seem to be a clear community understanding of our connection to the church" (GSC).

A majority of Chrs and almost half of the ECCs have been in existence for 11 years or more. But it appears that longevity does not, by itself, determine leadership style (although it is likely a factor). Chrs and ECCs are similar in that both display a considerable range in leadership selection styles (17 percent elected, 21 percent by discernment, 30 percent volunteers, 17 percent unstructured in ECCs; 5 percent elected, 48 percent by discernment, 14 percent

Table 32
How Leaders Designate Process

Designation	GSC	H/L	Chr	CTA/ECC	
Volunteer	45%	48%	15%	43%	35%
Election	3	19	4	4	20
Discernment	18	15	50	15	26
Appointment	9	15	15	4	2
Little or no structure	25	3	17	34	17

volunteers, and 19 percent unstructured in Chrs). Within both of these groups, the number of women and men leaders is roughly balanced (23 percent women and 26 percent men in ECCs; 40 percent women, 35 percent men in Chrs). In both the percentage of unstructured communities is about the same (17 percent in ECCs; 19 percent in Chrs).

There are differences as well in these two types. ECC leaders are twice as likely to be volunteers, and Chr leaders are twice as likely to be chosen through a discernment process. Factors other than group longevity are likely to account for the differences. For example, we know from the motivation survey that ECC members are sensitive on issues of dominance/power. "Well, there is really no formal leadership structure, nothing written down, or anything like that. I think we have gone out of our way not to have a hierarchical type of structure" (ECC). It may be that this sensitivity inclines these groups to shy away from structures of designated leadership, preferring volunteer responsibility, or leaving things even more fluid. And in Chrs, the preference for leaders named through discernment processes may well reflect their religious/ideological commitment to acknowledging the action of the Spirit within the community. In the interviews, a connection between prayer and discernment is frequently mentioned.

Among H/L communities, over half (60 percent) have been in existence five years or less, and almost half (47 percent) report volunteer leadership. Yet leadership in H/Ls appears to be somewhat more defined than in CTA and GSC groups, even though the percentage of volunteer leadership is high (over 40 percent in all three).

Only 5 percent of H/Ls report no structured leadership, while that is the case with 36 percent of CTAs and 24 percent of GSCs. The more defined leadership in H/Ls possibly reflects a higher level of episcopal and institutional support. In a 1996 Pastoral Plan for Hispanics, U.S. bishops gave formal approval to the development of SCCs, and a guideline booklet has been published. Support ministry is coming into place to sow the seeds of H/L communities.

Rotating Leadership—Revolving Responsibility

Our questionnaire about leadership style did not include rotating leadership or revolving responsibility as an option that could be checked. However, a number of people wrote one or the other in as an alternative to the listings we provided. And we know from interviews and transcriptions of meetings that one fairly common pattern is that the gathering place moves from home to home, and that someone from the week's meeting house plans the gathering and leads it. "We meet in different houses and whoever is the host, she is the one who will choose the readings and coordinate. That means that all of us are *faciladores*" (H/L). "I think in most places…the leader becomes the person with the largest house, and can host, can invite people to their house" (H/L). Interestingly, this evokes the pattern of the early church in which the house host also became the community leader.

These situations invite interpretation. The fluid pattern of revolving responsibility may imply a desire for participative or democratic structures, reflecting the cultural ambiance of SCCs in the U.S. Catholic Church. And it may also simply reflect the time constraints that many Americans experience because of busy life styles (identified as an SCC *problem*), leaving members reluctant to assume the continuing responsibilities of a leadership term.

An equally plausible explanation may be the early stage of group development of most SCCs in the study. Groups mature as relationships develop between members and between the group and others outside the group. One of the indications of a maturing group is its increasing ability to be explicit about the flow of power in its life. Groups mature through conversations about power: how initiative and influence, social control, and accountability will function in the community. Longevity is not the only factor, but it is a contributing factor in group maturity. Power issues exist in *every* group, and the ability to address them explicitly is a sign of community growth—even a *condition* of community development. Rotating leadership, then, may imply that in these relatively recent SCC groups, power remains an acknowledged *and* threatening topic of open conversation. Leadership, then, becomes a so-called hot potato that must quickly be passed around. In such cases not much group nourishment results, but no one gets burned.

Concerns involving dominance/domination reported explicitly among ECCs, and to a lesser but noticeable extent in CTAs, may reflect a suspicion that structured leadership could succumb to the temptation of unilateral uses of power. The desire in these two groups to have SCCs serve as an alternative to the current institutional forms of church gives weight to this interpretation of skirting power issues.

It may also be that revolving responsibility is less a resistance to the dark side of social power and more a lack of confidence in personal power. Since leadership is almost entirely lay, laypeople may sense themselves lacking in *religious* leadership ability in unaccustomed areas such as prayer, scripture, and spirituality.

Since the development of leadership skills in small Christian communities deserves sustained attention, we will return to this topic in chapter five.

Addressing Conflict

When communities were asked what was troublesome about community experience, about 10 percent of GSCs and Chrs cited the dominance of one person in the group or disagreement among members. Over 20 percent of ECCs cited conflict as being a problem. The interviews revealed a broad variation in comfort or discomfort with conflict, which is part of U.S. Catholic life generally.

When conflict was acknowledged, it tended to be focused in one of three areas: leadership, group decision-making, or discontent with the institutional church. At times, leadership conflict was generalized: A lay minister in a parish where an SCC was located had been summarily fired, causing tension and conflict in the small community as well as in the parish.

In the interviews, some members spoke explicitly about their dissatisfaction with leaders in the institutional church. "[My community] certainly made me feel much more aware of the variety of concerns that trouble people. I would not have been so aware if I did not hear the stories and see the pain that people experience as a result of pastoral indifference or pastoral abuse from the church" (CTA). Yet the SCC is precisely what allows some disenchanted people to remain connected. "Well, I would not keep interacting with the institutional church very much at all unless I had the support group to help me" (CTA). "The small faith community does what the parish used to do" (CTA). "I'm not really dependent on parish life at all anymore. In fact, it's more of an encumbrance....But for me, I find my spiritual nourishment in the small faith communities" (CTA). Comments like these are most likely to come from CTA/ECC members. The important thing is that people who have felt distanced from the institutional church for one reason or another (often around power issues) have stayed connected and active through their SCC. "It intensified my sense of belonging. Not necessarily to the universal church but certainly to my parish, and to my diocese to a certain extent. I have difficulties with the hierarchy, so when I'm talking about 'my church,' I am speaking mainly of my parish. And I get a lot of support from my parish and from my small Christian community" (CTA). In the national Catholic population, regular attendance at Sunday Eucharist is about 32 percent, which means that many people who used to be connected no longer are. It is plausible that some of these would find it easier to stay connected if they recognized SCCs as an alternative or additional experience. "I'm not as angry anymore since I found this community, and I don't feel as alienated....I used to think, 'Am I the only person sitting in the pews here that feels the way I do?'" (CTA) "Many of us are still in the church and in active ministry because of it [SCC]" (CTA). Since many of the citations here are from CTA communities, it is important to recall that CTA members are among the most active Catholics in parish ministries.

In these discussions, we could see a clear link between conflict and belonging: Tensions with the larger church set off questions about allegiance. Should we still call ourselves Catholic? One member observed that his group preferred to call itself *catholic* with a small "c."

Anger that is *not* acknowledged and processed is paralyzing, but anger that finds a legitimate outlet is capable of generating immense social energy for change. "We are fed up with things the institutional church is doing, but we want to reform it, not give it up and leave it" (ECC). Community organizations sometimes call this *sanctified anger* and identify it as the kind of energy that hope needs in order to operate. In his book, *Hope within History*, Old Testament scholar Walter Brueggemann names the exodus as an event that enables hope to operate. First, there must be a public cry of pain (Moses led the community in prayer, and aloud they poured out to God the pain of slavery). Private pain generates no social energy. Second, the community must know who or what is responsible for the pain (ideology critique). Only when these two things have happened is social and religious imagination generated: People realize that something else might be possible and are empowered to act. The critique of the church is most visible in the CTA/ECC communities. At SCCs, public expression of pain can occur. Perhaps because of this, they not only allow people to remain connected, but provide energy for transformative activity.

Often it seemed that the very intensity of belonging to this small, face-to-face group brought members into tension with what they felt was by contrast a more anonymous institutional church. "We just found parish life very deadly, and the liturgy deadly, and parish life was very empty. And so we experience the need for community because being Catholic is about community" (CTA). The small community is often referred to as being *like a family*, distinguishing it from the larger parish community of the diocese.

Stories of both success and regret in dealing with conflict appeared often in the interviews. One group had spent many months struggling to reach a consensus about a difficult choice it faced. When the decision was finally made by a majority, those who could not agree did not leave. "Instead," the interview reported, "we were still able to care for one another." But in another GSC community, growing tension around questions of morality caused one couple, longtime members of the group, to finally leave. Sadness at this turn of events was mixed with a determination to continue and to be more sensitive to differences within the group.

The explicit acknowledgment of conflict within their life of faith is a somewhat new experience for Catholics. Lively testimony in the interviews shows that small groups often permit and even provoke conflict. In these intimate settings, it is much less easy to disguise or ignore differences and disagreements.

SCC members were reluctant to admit to substantive conflicts in their shared life, opting instead to point to an external difficulty such as scheduling and time constraints, or to reply that their groups experienced no conflict.

I will add a reflection that does not stem from this research project, but from my contact with SCCs over the past 25 years. From time to time, I am asked whether there is any pattern in the reasons why communities cease to exist. (Our current research did not try to locate members of communities that no longer exist to ask for reasons.) I encounter two patterns. The first is that a community with no connection and activity beyond itself grows stale from internal preoccupation. But I would estimate that the more common reason is that communities fall apart through conflict avoidance. The inability of a community to deal with a dominant, controlling personality often leads to a community's extinction. I would put the development of skills in conflict management (or resolution) high on the agenda of leadership formation.

PART TWO:
SCCs—THE DIFFERENCE THEY MAKE

"It Matters!"

I return again to the answer given by the philosopher Alfred North Whitehead, when a student asked after class how he would characterize reality. The professor put his books back on the desk and stood for several minutes in silence, then replied: "It matters. It has consequences." Only that. Then he picked up his books and left.

Whatever is *here* matters because it's here, for whatever is here (or there) has consequences of some sort. This mattering is not just the aftermath of something's presence, but the import is its presence. Presence means having effects, whatever has a hold on our becoming through its effects. Though not intended as a philosophical comment, when Jesus (and the entire biblical tradition) says that "by your fruits you shall know them," a similar statement is being made.

As we, the theological and research teams, framed the study, we were interested in what impact SCCs are having on people's individual lives, on parish life, on church life, and on the world around us. We also recognized that the movement is too recent to sustain that kind of study (although I believe that SCCs are places for religious virtuosi to find a church home, which provides an important lodging place in Catholic life that religious communities used to offer).

What we are reporting on is how SCC members perceive the difference their membership has made to them. It is not always clear whether people get more involved in the parish because of their SCC, or whether people involved in the parish are the kind of Catholics more likely to join an SCC. But there certainly is a documentable connection one way or the other. Sometimes the causal relationship is stated: "I think everybody in the group has basically gotten involved in something that has to do with the parish" (GSC). In some instances we see them reflect on how SCCs have made a difference in a parish setting, but the assessment is through their perception, not that of the parish. Table 33 shows the stated claims.

All of the types indicate a significant influence of SCCs in increasing member interest and involvement in church life, civil life, or various issues. The most marked influence is clearly among the H/L communities. We did not ask directly: "How did membership influence work?" But the evidence is clear from interviews and SCC meetings. People bring their real lives into dialogue with scripture and with the other resources of the faith tradition. One member comments: "And that's why the perspective of social justice is so clear to me now, that no, the church is not a social welfare agency, but it has to be partly that. I mean, we have to be concerned with the common good" (GSC).

When we asked community members to name values that are very important to them, the social variety registered high (Table 34).

We should not be surprised by this time to see that CTA/ECC interest in political issues is greater than that of the general Catholic population. The other groups are roughly comparable. GSCs, H/Ls, and Chrs are significantly more likely (29–39 percent)

Table 33
The Impact of Community Membership

	GSC	H/L	Chr	CTA/ECC	
Has led me to become more involved in parish activities	67%	81%	67%	54%	33%
Has instilled a new sense of responsibility for parish and neighborhood	34	74	33	32	39
Has led me to be more involved in pro-life and family issues	39	49	67	27	18
Has led me to be more involved in civic and political affairs	26	22	37	57	57

Table 34
Social Values

Area of Concern	GSC	H/L	Chr	CTA/ECC		GRC/NG
Helping others	83%	81%	83%	88%	89%	73%
Parish	73	86	74	47	58	47
Political issues	24	25	20	32	47	26

than the general Catholic population to value interest in the parish. CTA/ECCs, the most critical of institutional Catholic life, are closest to the general population in this value. All of the SCC groups are in the 80th percentile in valuing help given to others.

When we questioned members about activities that were part of every gathering, we included three social areas: responding to needs within the group, helping others outside the group, and social or political issues (Table 35).

Table 35
Regular Active Expressions of Social Concern

Concerned about	GSC	H/L	Chr	CTA/ECC	
Helping SCC members	23%	31%	17%	19%	27%
Helping others in need	16	21	12	18	27
Political, social issues	8	19	2	25	21

We have often encounteed commitment to social issues among the ECC communities, and that shows again. About a fourth of ECC communities are concerned with social issues at every meeting. Among the three largest SCC types, the H/L communities are more likely than the others to attend to social concerns at every meeting. That would certainly reflect their own struggles with poverty and education, as the data for their profile indicate.

The picture that emerges is that most people in SCCs are concerned with social issues, even if the groups do not put those energies to work. They tend to focus more on people's needs than on systemic issues, probably indicating that many do not see the connection between human needs and dysfunctional social systems. And while SCCs lead many to a deepened interest, the communities do not tend to respond to need as a community. As one member states, "We leave it up to individuals to act on their faith. We don't act as a group" (GSC).

Social concern is most visible in the motivations and attitudes surveys, but there is less evidence of common social action beyond the group. SCC members may well support or even develop personal commitment to care for the needs of others and awareness of the systemic roots of injustice, but the description of SCCs as both gathered and sent (i.e., sent vis-à-vis their SCC life) seems to lie beyond the self-understanding of most SCCs in the U.S. Catholic Church.

A Type-by-Type Reprise

In chapters three and four we have looked at the people who join small Christian communities, their reasons for joining and for remaining, their regular activities, and the impact that their experiences have had on them and their world. It will be helpful here to characterize them group by group.

GSC—General Type of Small Christian Community

The data indicate that 60 percent of the GSCs have participated in RENEW, and that for over a third of the communities, RENEW had much to do with their interest in being part of an SCC. GSC members say that through their community they have received spiritual nourishment, a new way of being in a parish, and, in fact, a new way of being church.

A third of these communities said that their main reason for joining was to learn more about their religion, scripture, and the church. Social support was the second named reason, the desire to make new friends and to have fellowship. Once they are into community, they say that sharing and fellowship are their highest reasons for remaining members.

A recurrent theme among this group was not just to understand their faith better, but to struggle to live out that faith in the context of today's challenges. So a question that emerges from the group is: "Are we reacting Christ-like? We can't pretend to know and love Christ or follow him and then all of a sudden really go ballistic about something" (GSC). Their critical reflection leads them to realize that "the church isn't out there. Christ is not out there. Christ is here. We try to live better today and we draw our strength from each other so that we can make good decisions. Within the church is a caring, sharing group trying to live out their faith in the ordinary struggles of daily life" (GSC).

The openness to the challenge of actually living out one's faith and the risk that these people take in sharing their troubles, their obstacles, their sufferings, as well as their hopes and dreams—all of these help them move beyond the particularity of their lives to their sisterhood and brotherhood with all people. "After all this time together and the sharing of our pains and joys, we become aware that in the long run we are all human and we are all in it together" (GSC). While community members value the insight they gain into their faith, there is as well an affective need and desire to find a safe place: "It's nice to have a safe place just to come together…and to be able to cry" (GSC).

Tough subjects are addressed too. The things people share help them identify the sin they experience in their own lives and in the world. "God calls us to be somebody special and it seems that each sin takes us away from that call to be special and we become less. And each time we do something that makes us less, we give up our integrity and are dishonest, and [that] makes it harder for us to get back to the way we are called to be. And in all of this I can't get over how much we mean to God" (GSC).

Two of the most recurrent themes have been the impact GSC members feel at having developed their own articulation of their faith, and being able to identify their own voice. It is a confidence that does not just stay at the level of words; it is a confidence to be different and to act differently as people of faith. The second factor, a strength that seems to be developed through the intimate sharing of experience that often happens in communities, is transferable beyond just the immediate group. "There was a neighbor recently—we were friends and she was dying. She had cancer. I felt as though I needed to be with her even though we had not been close. I didn't know what I was going to say to her. She was dying. She was my age. But I did get involved with her. It happened just a few weeks ago. I just think this never would have happened, I never would have done this, years ago. I might have felt bad for her, but I would never have got on the phone and called her up and said 'I'm coming over.' Being part of my small base group helped me come to that confidence, helped me to break out of my fear, my awkwardness, to be able to reach out and care" (GSC).

Belonging to an SCC often enables members to be intimately present to those in pain, to *be there* when needed. "It's interesting that Jesus didn't pray for the disciples to be taken out of the world and preserved from contact with it. Jesus knew that the proper place for the disciples is in the world. That is what I learned from being part of our small group" (GSC).

H/L—Hispanic/Latino Communities

Something needs to be said about the term *Hispanic/Latino*. This designation was chosen because it seemed the most generic of the possibilities, but it does not do justice to the variety in communities. I have lived in both Texas and California, where most H/L people are of Mexican descent. Virgilio Elizondo has said that Mexican Americans in Texas increasingly think of themselves as mestizos and are increasingly claiming their Native American heritage. There are also significant numbers of Mexican Americans in the Upper Midwest, lured by work in harvesting. In New Orleans, where I now live, most of the H/L people are from Central America: Ecuador, Honduras, Guatemala, and Nicaragua. There are striking cultural differences between each, and between all of them and Mexican Americans. In Florida, New York, and other places along the East Coast, more of the H/Ls have a Caribbean background. Cubans and Puerto Ricans are present in large numbers. The cultural differences between these two are very significant, as are both of their cultures in contrast with the Mexican American heritage.

The vast majority of H/L communities with which we came into contact are Mexican American, and that needs to be kept in mind in the reflections that follow.

Like the GSCs, the Hispanic/Latino communities listed participation in RENEW as one of the factors most influential in their decision to join an SCC. About 70 percent said that learning more about religion and dedicating themselves to living the Word were *the* most important reasons for joining. Interestingly, H/Ls were the only community members to say that they joined to help their marriages or family life. And indeed, in the interviews H/L members cite the difference that membership has made on family life and marriage.

The H/L communities regularly included children on a large scale. Most H/Ls are intergenerational, reminiscent of the communities in the early church in which the entire *household* belonged (household then was larger than a blood-related family, or even a blood-related extended family). H/L members instinctively, culturally, tend to come with the whole family. At the close of this summary on H/L communities, I will offer some further thought on the cultural context of Hispanic/Latino families.

The H/L reasons for being in a small community are quite different from those of Anglo/Caucasian members:

- To improve my knowledge
- To know God better
- To learn more
- To enjoy friendships
- To bring my family into the church
- To be able to express myself

In a much more encompassing way than is true for any of the other groups, H/L communities constitute a huge part of both church life and the regular social life of members. The primacy of relationships is expressed and visible in practically all our interviews with members of H/L communities, "It is natural for people to come together...it is natural for them to come and help each other. Because they come to help each other, they come to know each other; they love each other. And they celebrate" (H/L). Their capacity for celebration is indeed notable.

Now, it is important to address nuances between the H/L communities we have studied and the others that are almost entirely made up of members with a European/American heritage. Dr. Jeanette Rodriguez says that there is little sustained reflection so far in U.S. Latino theology around ecclesiological issues, but that Dr. Gary Riebe-Estrella of the Chicago Theological Union is presently working in this area. His research has led him to identify an ecclesial model based on a sociological understanding of Latinos: They are sociocentric and organic in nature. This means that the fundamental unit of society is the group, or, more specifically, the family. The identity of the individual is anchored in membership in his/her group. Latinos (and others who are born and raised in this kind of social matrix) believe that it is not impossible to understand an individual in isolation from relationships. Rather, the individual is "regulated by strict rules of interdependence that are context specific and particularistic, rules governing exchanges of services, rules governing marriages, etc." (Schweder/Levine, 1984, 190).

This cultural perspective contrasts markedly with what is found in mainstream U.S. culture, which is characterized as egocentric and contractual. The individual is the basic unit, and the group happens through contractual arrangements. Persons in this context mature by distancing themselves from others in the process of individuation. The point is that the importance of family as a unit of membership in H/L communities reflects a profound cultural fact: The familial relationship is the fundamental model of all relationships. This relational model then extends through religious self-understanding and religious ritual. Being part of one's primary group and its interrelationships is not a matter of choice for Latinos; it is a given.

Charismatic Communities

Charismatics indicate a 75 percent satisfaction with participation in their groups. While the majority of communities reported little or no impact of their membership on attitudes toward the pope and church teaching, Chr and H/L members say that their membership has strengthened their loyalty. They also indicate that they have become more active in their parishes, and more concerned about pro-life issues.

Among Chrs, about half said that a main reason for joining is to come together with others for spiritual nourishment through praise, worship, and prayer. Less evident in other groups than among Chrs is a deference for personal conversion experiences. "Since I came down to prayer group, my whole life has been changed. It's not just a change. It's a new way of life. I can't be who I used to be, and I don't want to be. I can't be. It's just a completely new way of life guided by the Lord" (Chr). Chrs are also highly committed to weekly Mass attendance.

The personal experience of conversion fosters a threefold sense of mission: growth in holiness, building a loving community of peace, and a sense of evangelization. "In a way we came together as a small group on a weekly basis [to] talk and share and pray together...we don't want to turn in on ourselves...we want to reach out and evangelize" (Chr). "Out of gratefulness for what I experienced in these prayer groups, I decided to visit nursing homes. When I got there I was very aware of the smell. I didn't want to touch anyone. But because I was part of this prayer meeting, and because God touched my own heart, I got to the point where I am able to touch the people and let them touch me back. There is something that happened to me to help me get beyond the smell and cleanliness to acceptance" (Chr).

CTA—Call to Action Communities

Keep in mind that the communities we have designated as CTAs are identified that way because at least some of their members are active in the Call to Action organization. CTA does not designate CTA organizational sponsorship, or that all members belong to CTA. There are CTA characteristics, however, that are similar to the national organization. Members are often looking for alternatives— not *instead* of the institutional church but, rather, in addition to it. There is an articulated desire for a new way of being church. CTA and ECC communities have the best educated members, as well as the most critical and the most committed to social justice.

The interviews indicate a commitment on the part of many CTA members to find God in the world, which then leads to stronger commitments to social justice. "It [group membership and participation] allows me to find God in the events of the world. I think that if I weren't doing something to try to solve the church's problems, and the world's problems, I would probably not sense the wonder of what God is doing. Being active in those, in some way, has really helped me" (CTA).

The methodology of Catholic action, stemming from the influence of Cardinal Cardign, and common in Hispanic base communities, is often in evidence in CTA communities: see, judge, act. They name what they see. "It [my SCC] allows me to keep the broader world in mind instead of just getting swallowed up in the little world" (CTA). "I see things 'more knitted together'" (CTA). "We've become more self-aware as a group to what our issues are" (CTA).

The seeing leads to critical reflection and to action: "[I feel] a sense of being called to something bigger, a call really to be faithful and be committed" (CTA). "I got called…. My community called me to do things that I didn't think, didn't know there was a way of doing…. And you network with all of these people who [work at] it too. So it's a whole new model for creating, I think, new forms of ministry…we've got to go ahead and do it first before they will ever get the idea it can be done" (CTA).

ECC—Eucharist Centered Communities

Like the CTA communities, ECCs are interested in the transformation of the church and both keep their distance but also work assiduously for change, often by trying to model alternatives in their own community life. ECCs have the best educated and most affluent members of all the groups. They have strong interests in building community, in new forms of liturgy, and in freedom from the institutional church. In both CTAs and ECCs, members claim that their community experience has led many to become more involved in civic and political affairs.

CTA/ECC groups are committed to reform both within the church and within society. The mission statement that one ECC shared expresses what we saw and heard in many of the ECC communities:

> We, [name], are a small Eucharistic community rooted in the Catholic tradition. We are committed to the best of this living tradition, and are focused on the essential Christian message. Reading the signs of the times, we are responsible to a divine call to express our love through works of justice, compassion, and joy. We support one another on our spiritual journeys through creation-centered liturgies, faith sharing, and fellowship. Our community strives to:
>
> - welcome the divorced and remarried to sacramental life,
> - foster the equal ministry of women and men,
> - welcome children and single parents,
> - share a dialogue homily,
> - use inclusive language,
> - respect freedom of thought and reflection,
> - arrive at decisions through consensus,
> - have informal social gatherings and potluck brunches after Sunday Eucharist.
> - We welcome and accept all.

This mission statement embodies both the commitment and the challenge that tend to characterize CTA and ECC communities.

Some practices and convictions in both CTA and ECC communities run counter to the institutional church's self-understanding (and many more do not). In chapter five I will suggest the metaphor of *margins* for interpreting SCCs, which applies more fully to some than to others.

Summary

Most small Christian communities meet weekly or biweekly, a frequency that is important to the hold that SCCs have on members' lives. Most meet in members' homes, a more than merely incidental location. SCC members believe that what they are doing at home is being community and being church, and the location itself reminds them of the house churches that were the normative form of ecclesial life in the early centuries.

The four activities most common to all SCCs are prayer, faith sharing, scripture, and spirituality. Prayer helps bond the group into a community, enacts participants' connections to their Catholic heritage, and for many legitimates their SCC as a Catholic or religious activity (more than just a support or discussion group). Faith sharing is similar to what we believe is in fact theological reflection. It often involves people sharing with their community what is going on in their experience and how they find evidence of God's presence in the events of their lives. In SCCs people are able, without embarrassment, to discuss their efforts to be faithful, or perhaps even to be *holy*, though most would never use that word. One of the most important aspects of SCCs is scripture, in a church whose identity has been more self-consciously doctrinal than biblical. SCCs resonate with Vatican II's reappropriation of scripture as central to Catholic life. The process of sharing faith and experience aloud is critical to the appropriation of biblical meanings into Christian living; connections are made and implications are experienced. Spirituality does not seem to be a separate topic, but rather involves the intention and tone of all of the communities' activities, where people find their spiritual needs addressed.

Most SCC members value concern for human needs and say that membership has increased this concern. But SCC activities that implement social concern, especially beyond support needs within group membership, are not common. This is an area that should be open to growth.

SCCs report few formal structures of leadership. Having volunteer leaders or revolving responsibility is quite common. This might be because the majority of communities have come into existence fairly recently and may not have matured sufficiently to be explicit about the flow of power in their lives—or it may be that power remains a yet-to-be acknowledged and still-threatening topic of conversation. Attention to leadership formation should be on the agenda of SCC development. Leadership in community life does not appear to be strong.

The conflict that SCC members experience over church behavior and church issues is more explicitly acknowledged than that within communities. Stories abound of both success and regret in the handling of conflict. Overall, we do not perceive a readiness to address conflict head-on, and the lack of skills in conflict resolution is probably a big part of the reason. Education in conflict-resolution skills is recommended as part of the leadership formation that needs to take place.

Across the board, members are clear and enthusiastic about the impact that SCCs have on their lives. Because of their membership they are more involved in parish life and have a stronger sense of their obligation to respond to need. While SCC life does seem to deepen social awareness (especially through scripture), attending to social issues is not high as an activity of the community itself.

What does come through clearly is that for many SCCs, their relationship with the church is being reshaped. The fact that SCC membership is already largely an exercise of lay responsibility for faith was far less evident in the preconciliar church.

SCCs are moving scripture into a central place in their spirituality. The structured occasion to relate scriptural meaning to lived experience through a group process is utterly crucial. Faith sharing activities also encourage SCC members to be more explicit about the meaning of being Catholic. "It's not just being Catholic for the sake of being Catholic, but what does that mean in practice?"(GSC)

Another members observes that SCCs are "our personal story in the church." As a result of explicit attention to church issues, many members become more critical of the church, but also practice a greater sense of charity toward it. One member comments that the SCC "has helped me deepen my understanding of being Catholic...it's also helped me understand what I challenge in the Catholic organizational structure" (GSC). It is important to remember that a perceptive critic is one who examines and makes informed judgments about what is good and what is not. Some of the interviews suggest that SCCs do indeed promote both a critical spirit *and* a realistic commitment to the church.

5

Perspectives and Portents
Theological Interpretations
and Pastoral Recommendations

Introduction

Because there is no such thing as uninterpreted *fact*, the presentation of the research on small Christian communities—quantitative data, interviews, and meeting transcriptions—has involved interpretation all along the way. Even the gathering of data reflects the interests and concerns of the theological and research teams. But what follows is a more deliberate attempt to reflect interpretively on the picture of both small church communities and the larger church that emerges from the research. We have a double concern: to interpret the present situation accurately and offer suggestions (e.g., the need for leadership development), and equally to sense what kinds of portents SCCs are for a postconciliar, postmodern church in the making, and to offer suggestions (e.g., developing new parish models in which the kinds of conversation taking place in SCCs can shape community life and experience at the parish level). Interpretations offered here are for the most part theological, but built upon and responsive to the data, the interviews, and the observations offered in the earlier sections of the book.

At the beginning of this chapter, I offer the metaphor of *margins* to locate small Christian communities in the contemporary Catholic Church. On a page from a book, the margins are the open space on all sides of the text. But if anyone scribbles thoughts in the margins, it's hard to read the printed text as if there were no comments. I will

117

suggest that SCCs are like jottings in the margins of a text, where *text* means *the church*.

The Metaphor of Margins

For reasons that I hope will be clarified by the reflections that follow, I wish to claim that small Christian communities are important scribblings in the margins of a text called *church*. In the sense I want to use it, *marginal* complements a society that is alive and on the move. Strong, lively societies need marginal activity where the new is being tried out. It is my hope and guess that SCCs will be integrated into ecclesial self-understanding and will lose much of their marginal character at some point (in which case we can begin to wonder what the next scribblings in the margins will look like).

As both a hermeneutical and sociological category, I propose that margins is useful for exploring how small Christian communities are affecting people's reading of church, even the church's reading of itself.

I experience some initial hesitation about using margins as an analytical category. In popular usage marginal sometimes means irrelevant. But margins are always *on the page*, always *frame the text*, and anything written in the margins inevitably *conditions how anyone ever after reads the text*. Because of this last point, what is in the margins sometimes finds its way into the text in a new edition.

Margins as a Hermeneutical Metaphor

Hermeneutics is a theory of interpretation. I am suggesting that what appears in the margins influences any reader's interpretation of the main text. In the reader's mind at least, what is in the margins already impinges on the text, and perhaps even enters into the text.

How marginal life is identified in this book assumes that margins are absolutely critical to the growth of a tradition and the health of a community. John Meier's acclaimed 1987 book is called *A Marginal Jew: Rethinking the Historical Jesus*. The Jesus movement began as a marginal movement within Judaism. The prophetic voice has always been a marginal voice, forcing its way into the text and into the community.

How metaphor is being explored in this book is provoked by the Jewish philosopher/poet/mystic, Edmond Jabes, especially in *The Book of Margins;* and by the seminal anthropological work of Victor and Edith Turner, and reported by Victor Turner in his book, *The Ritual Process* (Edith Turner has been a member of our research team); and by the constructive interpretive use of these categories by theologian Terry Veling in his book, *Living in the Margins: Intentional Communities and the Art of Interpretation.* Veling is insistent that living *in* the margins, not *on* them is his interpretation.

Think of the church as it actually exists now, especially in its institutional self-understanding, as the written text on the page. And think of whatever postconciliar, postmodern church is coming into existence as a not-yet-written text. The margins, then, are the spaces where the unwritten text begins to interrogate the written text.

We are all familiar with scribblings in the margins of a borrowed book. It is not possible to read the page *innocently*. Marginal writing impinges upon the written text. Were the marginal scribbler not interested in the text, there would have been no scribbling. But the scribbler also feels *something else needs to be said* that the text doesn't say. The scribbler is both insider and outsider (Veling, 1996, 136).

Small Christian (or church) communities have sometimes received warm support from the bishops and pastors of parishes, and sometimes they have not. Rome has expressed reservations about liberation theology and basic ecclesial communities through Cardinal Ratzinger, and SCCs are praised and their contributions noted by Pope John Paul II in *Redemptoris Missio.* Therein is some institutional ambivalence about marginal activity. SCCs do not have a structured, legitimated ecclesial location or a specified relationship to parish or diocese. They have no juridical character. The fact that some bishops and pastors are supportive and welcoming does not create a juridical home for the SCC. Pope John Paul II acknowledges that they can be important instruments of evangelization, and that they help to decentralize a parish by spreading out responsibility for the community's life more widely among the community's members (*Redemptoris Missio,* §51). Still, they are not the way most parishes in the world, or in this country, conduct parish life. That is why I consider them, at this point, both marginal and of towering importance.

Margins is, of course, a page metaphor. In medieval manuscripts, the margins are often filled with images and scribblings, and recent scholarship takes them seriously as places where meaning is created. In his book, *Image on the Edge: The Margins of Medieval Art*, Michael Camille says that margins often do not create meaning by reference to specific texts, but by the story they tell in linked motifs and signs (Camille, 1992, 29). The general tendency of small Christian communities to do what they do in people's homes, and feel that they are being church there, is like the chain of linked motifs.

At other times, marginal material does relate directly to something in the text. Camille shows a manuscript from a *Book of the Hours* with a man in the left-hand margin who has made his way up the edge of the text. With his left hand he is pointing to a place in the text. In his right hand is a rope that goes to the bottom of the page and is attached to some text. The message is that marginal writing at the bottom of the page should be inserted into the text at the place where his hand points (Camille, 24).

I would say that scripture, for example, plays a prominent role in the life of SCCs that is hard to find elsewhere in Catholic culture as a consistent pattern of ritual life. SCCs are asking: "Is there not a way in the text called church of regularizing this practice in ecclesial life?" The kind of appropriating that occurs in a small community's theological reflection (whether they call it that or not) cannot occur in even the best of homilies, because the active participation of the community in fashioning the appropriation occurs only in committed and sustained conversation, and because no homilist can make strong, felt connections between scripture and the broad range of age and experience in the assembly. Because these communities are developing new models for connecting faith and experience, and because they are on the page, albeit often in the margins, they are beginning to create some new readings of the text called *church*.

Margins are a place where one can play with possibility. Camille observes that instincts are usually at work that keep play outside of narrow definitions, but within some sense of the larger scope. "Marginal images never step outside (or inside) certain boundaries. Play has to have a playground, and just as the [manuscript] scribe follows the grid of ruled lines, there were rules governing the playing fields of the marginal images that keep them in place" (Camille, 22). The large openness of SCC members to married priests is outside the present dispensation, but within the larger tradition. They are playing on a wider historical playground. The occasional presiding of those who have left the active priesthood and married is a further example. "Things written or drawn in the margins add an extra dimension, a supplement, that is able to gloss, parody, modernize and problematize the text's authority while never totally undermining it. The center is…dependent upon the margins for its continued existence" (Camille, 10). Victor Turner's work elucidates Camille's last comment, that the center needs the margins.

A Sociology of Margins

Sociologists understand well that any strong and interesting social organization has marginal activity, which in crisis times increases. As important as marginal life may be, it is seldom welcomed by life at the center, for it has the power to disrupt, that is, to suggest a different reading.

In his study of cultural change, Victor Turner notes the difference between *societas*, the large organizational unit, and *communitas*, the small units within the large. *Societas* attends, as it must, to structure and organization, to continuities and survival. *Communitas* deals with the inner life of the group, their needs, hopes, and aspirations, and is the *societas*'s contact zone with the ordinary, daily world. In periods of stability, the *communitas*'s identity with *societas* is easy and smooth. But in times of great change, the *communitas* does some distancing from societal structure and begins, on its own, to experiment with alternatives that are better suited to newly perceived needs. This is what Turner calls the antistructure dimension that is operative in the liminal period of change and new development. The marginal people, the *edgepersons*,

> who strive with passionate sincerity to rid themselves of the clichés associated with status incumbency…. *Communitas* breaks in through the interstices of structure, in marginality; and from beneath structure, in inferiority….Exaggeration of

structure may well lead to pathological manifestations of *com-munitas* outside or against the "law." *What is certain is that no society can function adequately without this dialectic....* [People] are released from structure into *communitas* only to return to structure revitalized by their experience of *communitas....*In liminality, the underling comes uppermost....Prophets and artists tend to be liminal and marginal people. (Turner, 1969, 102, 128, 129, *passim*, emphasis added.)

Those comments make it easy to understand why the institutional church has been both welcoming and wary, both supportive and challenging. These communities experience some autonomy because they are marginal and have no juridical status—yet they are clearly Catholic and willingly and loyally attached to that identity. The research data clearly support this judgment.

Turner's typology leads me to venture two connected judgments. First, I estimate that the appearance of SCCs all over the world is an example of *communitas* in a liminal period of serious, far-reaching social transmutation. It's where the new is being tried out, some of which will survive, or, in Turner's words, will "return to structure revitalized by their experience of *communitas.*" Some experimentation, of course, will not be incorporated into future structure.

Turner observed that those who were out of power in the last dispensation have a major role to play in creating the new one. They do not usually do this by taking up central positions in the authority structure, but by creating the agenda that the institution has no choice but to address. The people out of power in the Catholic Church have been the laypeople of God, generally, and laywomen especially. Both the membership and the leadership of SCCs is almost entirely lay, and the majority of leaders are women (by about the same proportion as women and men in SCC membership).

We have seen the kind of loyalty to church that characterizes most SCC members who are prayerful, churchgoing Catholics. This is their anchorage in Catholic culture and tradition, and I am going to presume the continuities that constitute this anchorage. I will emphasize, therefore, in no particular order, the liminal or marginal aspects of SCCs that may be portents about the church of tomorrow.

Second, it is my guess that when we have reached the other side of current institutional conversion, SCCs will lose much of their liminal character, but will have been constituted as normative structures in the next ecclesial dispensation.

Let us ponder then how SCCs might contain portents about the future of the U.S. Catholic Church.

Being Catholic Is about Community

Community is certainly a loaded word. You can talk about a neighborhood community, the Western community of nations, or the African American community as a way of categorizing. Earlier, we identified what the word *community* meant in the expression *small Christian community*. I would like to offer some descriptions of the word from the Judaeo-Christian and Catholic tradition to note an important gift of SCCs to contemporary Catholicism.

It was clear to our Hebrew forebears that God elected a people into covenant, and that redemption came to one through membership in the community. No Jew had a relationship with God independent of the community. Gerhard Lohfink's study, *Jesus and Community*, reminds Christians that Jesus proclaimed and initiated the kingdom of God, and that the healings and reconciliation that people experience happened to them, not without the love and compassion of Jesus, to be sure, but because God's reign was taking hold through Jesus' preaching and work. Healing happened because God's reign brings healing to the people among whom the kingdom of God takes hold.

The invitation to someone to become a disciple, "Follow me," was an invitation to join a community and to have a relationship with Jesus, *and* with a group of disciples. Paul's letters are full of his recommendations about how members of the community are implicated in each other's life, and how they must treat each other because they are members of the one body of Christ. Paul's word for community is *koinonia*, a Greek word whose root meaning is participation. The Greek word for *one another (allelon)* appears over 40 times in Paul's letters.

The individualism that is such a characteristic of American culture does not lend itself to the communal impulse that belongs radically to members of the body of Christ. There are, of course, communitarian impulses that have been and are operative in U.S.

culture. But they do not have a large presence. For most active U.S. Catholics, the Sunday Eucharist is their experience of gathering. It is not uncommon for a Catholic to attend Sunday Mass and not know the people on either side, in front, or in back—in which case, we do not experience ourselves as part of a community that has cho- sen to gather in celebration of what God is doing *among us* together. We do speak of the family as a domestic church, but it is a rare fam- ily in which this consciousness is a serious regular presence. It is an even rarer family that has activities which spring from that realiza- tion, and ritual with which to note it and celebrate it.

Having said all of that, *community* is a precious word and com- modity in Catholic culture, and it functions somewhat that way in American Catholicism. We owe a debt of gratitude to religious communities of women and men who have been a deliberate, highly visible presence of community. I believe that small Christian com- munities are offering Catholic lay culture a deliberate presence of community, with culturally transformative potential.

When Michael Cowan and I were working on the manuscript for *Dangerous Memories* in the mid-1980s, we chose to speak of SCCs at that time as ICCs, *intentional Christian communities*. A usage later developed that we did not intend, that ICCs were com- munities *without* a parish connection, and SCCs were communities *with* a parish connection. What we were trying to describe with the term *intentional* is the deliberate choice people must make to be committed to and interactive with a specific group for community to happen. Most people are not deliberately connected with the other people who come to Sunday Eucharist. They are seldom there with other community members with whom, in quite specific ways, they have struggled to be active, faithful disciples of the good news of Jesus Christ—people with whom they have shared precious things. *Intentionality* functions in any genuine community.

Eucharist is many things, one of which is a community's cele- bration of how the paschal mystery has shaped and transformed them in ways that make them glad—individually and collectively. There is a powerful eucharistic truth when the community that has experienced this gift gathers to name its experience of that gift and celebrate it. When that is the case, there is palpable content to the community's Amen. The body of Christ that the community has experienced itself to be and the body of Christ that comes to the community through bread broken and cup shared collude in wonder, silence, and song—in gathering and in sending.

When Paul scolds and instructs the community in Corinth (1 Cor 11), he is unhappy about their behavior *before* the Eucharist. People with means have better food and do not share it. Others have had too much wine. They do well when the agape is over and they turn to the Eucharist. When Paul scolds them for not recognizing the body of Christ, he does not mean that they fail to understand the reality of the bread broken and the cup shared. Instead, he means they have not recognized the body of Christ that *they* are. There is something they must be together before Eucharist that gives Eucharist its full power.

Anything that provides a structure for deepening the assembly's reality as community (you don't need to be a community to assemble) is a gift to parish life generally, and to eucharistic life, specifically. Thus, much seems right in the agenda of the National Alliance for Parishes Restructuring into Communities. In this model, communities are not just a parish program. They are meant to become a structural component of the church's ministry and celebration so that the dynamics just described are hospitably housed in the parish.

I propose an analogy. The recovery of local ecclesiology was a major move for Vatican II (still clearer in theory than in practice). Every local church is truly church. Dioceses are not administrative units of the Vatican. The authority of the leaders of the local churches, the bishops, derives from their authentic leadership of an authentic local church. The bishop's authority is not delegated authority. For full, authentic churchhood, local churches must, of course, be in union with each other and with the church of Rome, as must their leaders. Local churches are the building blocks of the universal church, which is more than the sum of its parts. However, without the parts it would not exist.

In the interviews, we sometimes heard community members connect their experience with that of the Pauline church. "Yes, I think we are a new way of being church—but a new way that is very ancient in our tradition. That's what's been exciting to discern, that Paul wrote these letters to small house churches" (GSC). I don't want to play this card more strongly than it deserves because these SCCs are not, of course, full-fledged local churches, nor even close. That's why I spoke of an analogy. But they are genuine Christian communities with churchhood about them. They gather shared memories and hopes, and build a collective experience whose character they trust. They author some Christian life together and trust the authority of what they author.

One SCC member spoke about his sense of being saved as a member of people, and that this came to him through discussions in his community. One day, two well-dressed young people knocked at his door and asked whether he confessed Jesus as his personal savior. He said: "Not exactly, but I confess Jesus as my communal savior" (GSC). One of the two shrugged and asked: "Would you say that again, please?" He said: "God makes a covenant with a people, and I am a member of a people with whom God has made a covenant through Jesus Christ. So Jesus Christ is my communal savior." One of the two at the door turned to the other and said: "Let's go!"

The experience of Christian life as necessarily and deeply communal is a retrieval being undertaken by SCCs in the U.S. Catholic Church. For anyone to know that a Christian identity is radically communal, something such as SCCs and/or the regular dynamics of SCCs appears to be essential. There may be other ways to know and live that communal dimension. But SCCs are a way that is happening, working, and creating precedents in communality (for example, they are creating new models for the experience of community).

Small Christian Communities and the Reign of God

Jesus preached the reign of God before there was a church. Vatican II recognized that the reign of God is larger than the church. The reign of God is a defining reason for the church. In some ways it is less the case that *the church has a mission* than that the *reign of God has a mission*, and it has a church for the sake of the mission.

Vatican II's document on the laity recognizes that the laypeople of God, from their baptism, have the right and the duty to engage in the church's sometimes internal mission (§3). "Promoting Christian friendship among themselves, they help one another in any kind of necessity" (§4). Mission includes equally the transformation of culture and, the social structures that we create and which create us. "Outstanding among the works of this type of apostolate is that of Christian social action" (§67).

Two things are clear from our research data. The first is that most members of SCCs are conscious of social commitment and value it. The second is that SCCs do not yet engage significantly as a community in Christian social action. The needed development involves bringing the experience of our social worlds into the conversation with faith as effectively as we bring in individual experience. For this to be effective, skills in social analysis are needed and are, in fact, true components of prayer form in this context. Practical theology, the mutually critical conversation between interpretations of faith and of our social worlds, a conversation that generates Christian praxis, is itself a spirituality. Habitually engaging in such conversation is a spiritually charged way of being Christian. In our judgment, there is need for more self-aware theological reflection. The habits of doing this are not firmly ingrained in the U.S. SCC character. But there are inklings of it. Some of it does happen.

In his theory of language, Jürgen Habermas coined an expression that, as awkward as it is in English, provides a strong insight into the character of Christian community that I have been trying to describe: *intersubjective communicative praxis.* People interact with each other in words, and in so doing decide what kind of a world or what kind of life they choose to make together, and what kind of praxis will get it done. The power of an SCC is precisely that it provides a manageable-sized group of people who interact with each other and with their faith. Discussing the world they want to exist, they can also talk themselves into whatever praxis is needed to make that world happen. "It's one thing to hear the Word of God, but to be able to talk about it, and share about it, and how it applies to your daily life among your peers, it's so different. It's more life-giving and enriching. So, yeah, it's really important" (CTA).

This is a distinct type of conversation that can happen only with a particular set of dynamics in a group of manageable size. It is not a likely kind of conversation at the level of parish, at least if it has not been going on in smaller groups numerous enough that their presence is a feature of parish culture. Nor is it the kind of conversation that normally constitutes the culture of a family, that is, a domestic church.

One interesting feature of SCCs is that even when connected to the parish, the community leadership is almost entirely lay—a different social location in which to have conversation about the Word and the world. Those who are poor will interpret the state of the economy differently than those who are affluent, because they have different social locations and therefore different perspectives and vested interests. Lay Catholics are in the world differently than ordained Catholics (different social locations). The institutional church knows that the laity are its privileged contact zone with society and culture (cf., especially *Gaudium et Spes* and *Apostolicam Actuositatem*). We believe that SCCs are one key way in which a contact zone with society nourishes the whole church's appraisal of mission.

Catholicity and Churchhood

The vast majority of SCCs have come into existence during the past five years, and most are in the GSC category. Their members primarily are over the age of 50 and better educated and better off than the average U.S. population. This strongly suggests that the SCCs of this population are the activity of a Catholic generation that has come of age in the United States and has been assimilated into middle-class and professional cultures. But this class of people wants to remain Catholic and seeks a venue that allows for discourse, community, and growth that can bind it to its Catholic heritage in a new way. (In a minority of cases the SCC allows persons to leave an institutional Catholicism that they find untenable, but remain connected with a community that has been shaped by Catholic culture.) In the process, these Catholics who have shifted their social location from ethnic enclave and working class to suburb and professional class are relating to their theological heritage differently. Data suggest that they are not being *Protestantized* but rather that they are becoming adults as laity in the U.S. Catholic Church.

For most SCCs the better interpretation is that these groups replace the extended families and neighborhoods of an earlier time as mechanisms for transmitting and maintaining faith. As denominational affiliation has declined as an ascriptive factor in the lives of people in the United States, new mechanisms for maintaining and transmitting the faith must emerge for denominations to continue to exist. SCCs are a creative response to this need.

In Chr groups, interview and observation data suggest some contact with writings in the Catholic theological heritage as well. Also in some GSC and CTA groups individuals talk about the books they are reading (e.g., Richard McBrien's *Catholicism*). We do not have sufficient interview and observation data to make hard conclusions here, but what we have does support the tentative conclusion that SCC activities transmit Catholic heritage in a way that allows it to ground self and social critique and to fund SCC members' imaginations for dealing with the challenges of their lives.

It is ecclesiologically significant that most SCCs meet in people's homes. While small Christian community is the most common designation for these gatherings, *house church* also occurs, as well as references to the early household model of church. SCC members commonly presume that they are being church when they gather. For some (a small minority), house church is their only church—it keeps them connected: "Some of our community members no longer go to church...the small church is their church.... I don't think the small community has pulled them away from the larger church as much as some of their own experience of things that have gone on in the church" (GSC). For others, the SCC has helped them remain attached: "It's kept me connected...to the church in the larger sense.... I am 99 percent sure that would not have happened had it not been for the small community coming along when it did" (GSC). Another observes: "And so 'make church together' became our motto. We make church together a little differently. If people are going to maintain their affiliation and the celebration of their faith, they're gonna have to be 'little churches,' to use that stark terminology" (GSC). A person who has parish responsibility for SCCs emphasizes the ecclesiological implications: "I am the coordinator of small Christian communities in the parish. That's my only job. We have 600 to 700 people in small church communities. We call them small church communities precisely to develop an ecclesiology so that people understand it's not just a small group, but it's really church when they gather" (GSC).

Both the herald and community ecclesiological models, as developed in Avery Dulles' classic *Models of the Church*, elucidate the churchhood of SCCs. Most SCC gatherings give scripture a central role. The breaking open of the Word is a central dynamic, for many a primary identifying feature of their SCC life together. Second, as baptized Christians, they have responsibilities for both community life and mission (apostolate). Canon law assures Catholics the right to form associations for spiritual and apostolic purposes.

As the data presented earlier indicate, the desire for community is a major motivation—not just any kind of support group (although support is valued), but people gathered around the life and message of Jesus Christ, and being church. One SCC member referred to a handout at Mass in both Spanish and English that named five aspects of SCCs: scripture, community, faith sharing, service, and union with the church. Commenting on the last item, the member said: "The latter is to understand that the community is not just another group, but that it's the church making itself present in a home. That is very important" (H/L).

Reconstructing Relationship with the Church

Particularly when SCC members talk about sharing faith, the interview and observation data show that this activity not only makes real God's presence in members' lives individually and sometimes corporately, it also connects them to the larger church. Across all types of SCCs participants talked about themselves as church, as people of God: "Church is the people of God, I mean, that it can help us to give life to that tradition, going back to the Pentecost readings. Who was church then and who is the church now?... The church has to look like Jesus, and if the church doesn't look like Jesus then we've missed the boat somewhere" (GSC). "...these groups integrate us, a small little group, into the bigger church" (GSC).

Experiencing themselves within their SCC as church, as people of God, members' faith sharing and overall participation in the group lead them to increase their participation in the church. Church as people of God, note members, requires "us to take more responsibility individually for being church and for our relationships with God" (GSC). Being responsible in the group pushes one to be more responsible for the parish. It also increases members' affective connections to the parish.

Faith sharing pushes people to look at the meaning of being Catholic: "...it's not just being Catholic for the sake of being Catholic, but what does that really mean in my life and what does that mean in practice" (GSC). SCC participation helps each member "deepen my understanding of being Catholic" (GSC). It also increases members' sense of belonging to a larger church. The SCCs are "our personal story in the church" (GSC).

The data for GSCs and other types of SCCs show SCC members becoming more active and thoughtful about their participation in the church, whether defined as the SCC itself, the parish, the diocese, or the universal church. Generally, SCC members are both critical and compassionate toward the church, a stance that suggests deepening psychological and spiritual maturity on their part. In the CTA/ECC interviews and observations we see some individuals for whom the SCC substitutes for parish or other church affiliation. Still, even for most of these members being in an SCC supports their connection to the institutional church through parish.

Belonging, Allegiance, Identity

The revolution in religious faith begun in the reforms of Vatican II invites Catholics to a more active participation in their faith and to an exercise of responsibility for church as a community of faith. We learn that as adults we not only receive faith—it is also *something we must perform* in both the church and the larger community. Catholics are asked to live a more active faith life and to give greater attention to the role of conscience and religious experience. The appearance of small Christian communities has given Catholics a practical vehicle for this new expression of faith: Catholics pray together, read and discuss scripture, and talk face-to-face about the connections between their faith and their daily lives. "Only by the light of faith and meditation on the Word of God can one always and everywhere recognize God in whom 'we live and move and have our being' (Acts 17:28), seek God's will in every event, and see Christ in all human beings, whether they are close to us or are strangers" (*Apostolicam Actuositatem*, §4).

The revolution in religious identity that Vatican II inspired has brought about another powerful change, a wider sense of church. Until Vatican II, church (*real* church) tended to mean "other Catholics." Catholics now feel encouraged to see other Christians as partners rather than adversaries. Official Catholic vocabulary sometimes speaks of other Christian traditions as "the churches" rather than as "separated brethren." We often find ourselves called out to non-Christians as well in the civic community as potential allies in the pursuit of justice. Some SCCs have Christian members who are not Catholic, and that is not an issue for them.

As we have seen, the data indicate a strong and loyal attachment to the church on the part of SCC members, significantly stronger than among the general population of Catholics who do not belong to any kind of religious small group. Traditional Catholic identity has been closely allied with allegiance to the pope and to church teaching. However, SCC members, like the Catholic population in general, are feeling the tension between teaching authority and their own conscience and experience (less pronounced among Chrs, most pronounced among CTA/ECCs). This seems to signal a shift in the religious identity of Catholics that is relevant to the whole church. This was noted earlier, but not in the context of Catholic identity. In feeling invited to become more adult and responsible, Catholics have come to take seriously their allegiance to the internal authority of their conscience, especially when it has been shaped by their direct experience. Increasingly, the church will feel the pressure to make visible and convincing the material authority (the authority of evidence and reason) for positions put forth with formal authority. We have seen that need documented in relationship to education, and the level of education for Catholics is significantly on the rise.

Becoming more adult in their faith often means for contemporary Catholics a critical posture in the church to identify both what is working well and what needs to be transformed. These dispositions are apparent throughout the range of types of SCCs, but are most apparent in the CTA/ECC groups. The Call to Action movement is probably an expression of this disposition (and for some it is a disturbing presence).

As involvement and the sense of being Catholic increase, many SCC members become more critical of the institutional church but also practice a greater sense of charity toward it. One member talked about the ability "to honor it [institutional church] and yet to be able to stand back and have a critical voice too, and to try to talk that line" (GSC). Another commented that while the small community "helped me deepen my understanding of being Catholic…it's also helped me understand what I challenge in the Catholic organizational structure" (GSC). One used an image to express this combination of critical and compassionate awareness of the church: "…a snake takes seven years to change its skin, but underneath his new skin is growing so that when the old one is gone, there's a whole new one there. So I think somehow that's what's happening now in the church. As it probably has always happened, you know" (GSC). One woman put it this way: "No, I haven't become more critical because I think I have become more [aware] that all has to be figured in" (GSC). SCC members understand the life of their groups as dynamic, in process (GSC). Many come to appreciate the dynamic process as part of institutional church life as well. Additionally, one member commented that their group's "respect" for the pastor "is much greater than it would be had we not known him now as well as we do" (GSC).

The SCC experience clearly reinforces and supports Catholics' sense of belonging to the church. The English writer, Edmund Burke, once observed that a person only feels part of the larger batallion by first of all belonging actively and effectively (and I would add, affectively) to their "little platoon." SCCs seem to provide that connection and that deepening ownership of church life.

The Inner Life of Small Christian Communities

Leadership attends to a range of significant dynamics in group life, including initiative, task achievement, shared vision, and common mission. Across the SCC types, communities report initiative and achievement in many of their inner tasks, such as hospitality, mutual support, the planning of worship and of discussions, recruitment, and so forth. Rotating responsibility, a common leadership model, seems to serve these tasks adequately.

The leadership tasks of developing shared vision and focusing group resources for common mission are less evident. Since so many communities maintain a relationship with the parish, it may be that the parish serves some of the leadership functions. Perhaps some forms of leadership are expected from the parish rather than from the community. There may also be some expectation that issues of vision will be addressed by some of the national organizations with which many SCCs are affiliated.

We have already noted the large number of younger groups, especially in the GSCs, H/Ls, and CTAs. Conscious attention to effectiveness normally emerges later in a group's life (issues involving belonging, power, and intimacy develop first). Generating shared vision and focusing resources for some kind of common action or mission often occur, therefore, in more advanced stages of group maturity.

While these reasons are surely part of the picture, I believe that a more likely interpretation of what we perceive as a somewhat *flattened* leadership in SCCs is that internal leadership for vision and mission is not really sensed to be a requirement in a group that gathers primarily for *belonging*. The data tell us that belonging is a strong motivation for joining, and becomes an even stronger motivation for staying in the community. Thus, if SCCs meet primarily for worship, prayer, faith sharing, reading and reflection on scripture and its claim on members' lives, then a fluid sense among the community members of *who does what around here* would suffice. We would expect explicit leadership patterns to become more significant for a group only when shared vision leads to common action beyond the group itself.

The Participative Impulse

Sacrum Concilium, Vatican II's document on liturgy, asks for the full, active, conscious participation of all the gathered community. The small community offers a special opportunity for the implementation of this directive. It is a rare SCC gathering in which all present do not have some opportunity to speak and act. Liturgists, pastors, and presiders struggle to learn how to implement the call to full, active, conscious participation in liturgy in a gathered community as large as a normal parish's Sunday Eucharist. Perhaps the SCC phenomenon is a call to incorporate small community dynamics in large community celebrations. Of course, that is easier to say than to do. What full, active, conscious participation does is bring the intentionality of the group into ownership of the gathering and what transpires within it. And SCCs do seem to do that.

Responsibility for the shape of any gathering and for the configuration of regular community life tends to lie within the community. There is little indication of communities being over and against anything, nor of any desire to be autonomous and independent (the strongest assertion of independence would be in ECCs—but there, too, we find the most social justice activity, nourished by church teaching). Even though most communities (about three-fourths) are parish connected, primary leadership (even when weak) appears to rest within the community. Members participate in the decisions that give the community its character. I want to make this a measured statement, for I am not suggesting that these SCCs are idiosyncratic gatherings off on their own. Tradition shapes their living and meeting, and they network. Most members who attend Eucharist do so in their parishes. But there is some genuine agency that they experience that arises from their own initiative, and which occurs within their own sense of themselves as church. That is a form of participation not normally available in traditional church structures, and participation is a particularly strong appetite in U.S. culture.

SCCs offer a place where the community leadership of women is commonplace. More women than men attend church regularly. By about the same proportion, more women than men belong to, and are leaders of, small Christian communities. This latter piece of information is noteworthy because in the written text of the church no official leaders of communities are women. SCCs are led in prayer and theological reflection by both women and men. I am not interested in entering into ordination issues. Rather, I am simply indicating a phenomenon: that in SCCs women and men both lead communities in prayer, especially Liturgy of the Word, because they also lead them in the dynamics of their life. In his book on margins, Michael Camille notes that they "represent things excluded from official discourse" (Camille, 126). This would be an example—something that doesn't go away because official text does not include it.

The Community and Its God

In the interviews with SCC members we asked whether community experience had changed their understanding of God, grace, sin, redemption, and so forth. The questions did not draw much of a response. There is not, therefore, much explicit data. I believe, however, that some inference is warranted, very much in dialogue with an assessment of religious groups in Robert Wuthnow's *Sharing the Journey*. In support of such inference, I want to cite some SCC members' comments from interviews (and then refer to Wuthnow's assessment):

> ...when people are so tortured, if you will, with being abandoned, they must of necessity turn to a surrogate parent. And for me, this community of five or six becomes the surrogate community...where I can feel the wholeness of what Christ was trying to impart (CTA).

> ...she survived two years because of the support from this particular small Christian community. People really stood by her and helped her both spiritually and physically to get through the grief and suffering (GSC).

> This church here, this group, is constantly going through birthing...nurturing me with strength to stay on...a light for me in the midst of terrible darkness. This darkness is very much evidenced by the institutional church (CTA).

> I feel so much more at home and free to express myself, and comfortable.... It's just the freedom and the ease to share our experiences, faith experiences, faith sharing...and the wisdom you gain from [other] people's experience when they share those experiences (ECC).

The small Christian community is for many a place where they are comfortable being themselves, where they feel support in difficult times, where they can share their experience and hear other people's experience. There is relatively little testimony to *tough love*. My inference is that SCC members presume God is acting in and through these communities to give us support and to let us know we are loved.

Wuthnow states that

> ...there is a danger if God becomes a being with the same char-
> acteristics as those experienced in one's support group...spiri-
> tuality is domesticated at the same time that it is reinforced....
> Sacredness ceases to be the *mysterium tremendum* that com-
> mands awe and reverence and becomes a house pet that does
> our bidding. God becomes a source of advice and comfort, and
> the proof of God's existence becomes the group. Because the
> reality of the sacred depends on God's relevance to our lives,
> God becomes easier to understand and God's actions become
> smaller, modifying our attitudes and calming our anxieties,
> rather than moving mountains. But a domesticated view of the
> sacred has always been worrisome to the saints and the sages
> who have struggled most deeply with its meaning and implica-
> tions. And the possibility that small groups are encouraging
> this kind of faith is troublesome to at least some religious lead-
> ers today (Wuthnow, 1994, 231, 255).

The God of the prophets does not make a strong appearance
in SCCs. There is little divine fierceness. This is most certainly
related to the evidence that the support and sharing dimension of
SCC life looms much larger than the communities' public life in a
troubled world. "I feel so much at home and free to express myself,
and comfortable" (ECC). "It amazed me that I could sit with an
Attila the Hun, and I probably had nothing theologically in common with him, and yet we all loved each other and could respect
each other's point of view" (CTA). "There's a set of rules that we
established from the beginning. No one is to preach and no one is
to teach. We're only there to share, and whatever's said is accept-
able. You don't have to believe it, but you have to accept...that that
person believes it, and that's fine. So one person does not comment
on another person's views, opinions, or sharing" (GSC). Much of
this is indeed admirable and requires tolerance and refined listening
skills. But it can feed into the religious sensibilities about God that
Wuthnow describes above.

One way of saying what I want to say is that the prophetic
imagination about God and the world is not a strong presence in
the conversation and activities of most SCCs in the U.S. Catholic
Church. (The H/Ls we interviewed that are not privileged groups

are the exception.) Abraham Heschel's description of prophetic living captures the sense of things that are not strong in SCC life in this country.

> The situation of a person immersed in the prophets' words is one of being exposed to a ceaseless shattering of indifference, and one needs a skull of stone to remain callous to such blows.... Perhaps the prophet knew more about the secret obscenity of sheer unfairness, about the unnoticed malignancy of established patterns of indifference, than those whose knowledge depends solely on intelligence and observation.... The prophet's word is a scream in the night. While in the presence of God the prophet takes the part of the people. In the presence of the people the prophet takes the part of God.... The prophet is human, yet employs notes one octave too high for our ears.... Above all, the prophets remind us of the moral state of a people: few are guilty, but all are responsible! (Heschel, 1962, xii and chapter one, *passim*).

Heschel says that the prophet is not simply enraged at injustice (though that too), but rather has a close, personal relationship with God, knows what God feels about the world, and then feels the world with God's feeling. The fundamental experience of the prophet is a fellowship with the feelings of God, *a sympathy with the divine pathos*, a communion with the divine consciousness that comes about through the prophet's reflection of, or participation in, the divine pathos.... Prophets live not only their personal lives, but also the life of God. Prophets hear God's voice and feel God's heart.

The fact that most SCC members in the U.S. Catholic Church are educated and middle-class may make it more difficult to feel the pain that triggers prophetic imagination. But that fact does not free a community from its ability and its need—its spirituality—to feel the feelings of God. A romance with scripture helps nurture this kind of spirituality. What SCCs have going for them is that they are developing a strongly biblical spirituality. We are children of Isaiah, Jeremiah, Micah, Osee, and Amos even as we are brothers of Jesus and children of God. It remains to be seen whether the prophetic imagination will be able to take hold—whether theological reflection is able to include social analysis, and whether middle-class communities can make living, interpersonal contacts with those who exist on the edges and on history's underside. In a word, it remains to be seen whether the faith of small Christian communities can activate more vividly its public character.

The Public Life of Small Christian Communities

It is commonplace to observe that any truly ecclesial community is both gathered and sent, that it has an inner life and a public life. SCC attention is far more directed to inner life than to social issues. Now there is, to be sure, a mission *ad intra* as well as *ad extra*. The reign of God shapes our relationships with each other in the community's inner life. My focus here, however, is upon the need of SCCs in the U.S. Catholic Church to develop attention and response to the church's mission beyond the immediacy of SCC membership.

When Michael Cowan and I were preparing *Conversation, Risk, and Conversion* for publication, we made a judgment about which we felt strongly, but briefly considered omitting so as not to alienate those with whom we want to be in dialogue. This involved our having found resistance in workshops around the country to insistence that *being sent* is a constitutive feature of any community that considers itself to be church. The objection would go something like this: "In our eight years together we have prayed, listened to God's word, been present to each other's lives in celebration and in pain. We have been present to someone whose spouse of 30 years died of cancer, to parents when they learned their daughter was a lesbian, to new parents celebrating the baptism of their children, to the pain of separation and divorce, to one person dealing with chemical dependency. We have laughed and cried together. We have stuck in there, no matter what. You cannot tell me we are not community." I am proud of that kind of record and would not tell such a group: "You are not community." I would say, however, that if SCCs are, in the long haul, going to have a major impact on the formation of Catholic identity in the U.S. Catholic Church, they are going to have to take seriously their potential impact upon the evangelization of culture, that is on the structures that shape human life. Therefore, Michael Cowan and I expressed the following:

> Our judgment in this book, for gospel reasons and for socio-
> logical reasons, is that SCCs in this country will be a blip on
> the screen of ecclesial history rather than an engaging, strong
> narrative, if communities do not have a proactive conversation
> with the world beyond their community membership as well as
> effective mutual conversation with each other. Gathered and
> sent. The gathering does the sending. The sending calls for
> gathering. (Cowan/Lee, 1997, 11).

The Vatican II document on the laity could not be stronger on this point. Its title, *Apostolicam Actuositatem*, is difficult to translate into English. "Decree on the Apostolate of the Laity" catches the vigor of something more akin to "The Apostolic Actuality of Lay Life," as clumsy as that sounds. "Modern conditions demand that the lay apostolate be thoroughly broadened and intensified. The constant expansion of population, scientific and technical progress, and the tightening of bonds between people, have not only widened the field of the lay apostolate, ...these developments have [also] raised new problems which cry out for the skillful concern and attention to the laity" (§1).

The apostolic agenda of the church has been developed and articulated with extraordinary clarity and power by Pope John Paul II and by U.S. bishops as well. The theory is strong and clear, but concrete social praxis lags. The fact that a major dynamic of SCCs is precisely that faith and experience are drawn into active conversation opens the SCC to what needs to happen, that is, the experience dialoguing with the imperatives of faith be not just personal experience but social experience.

In his report on the multitude of small groups showing up in U.S. culture, Wuthnow expresses concern about groups' preoccupation with internal concerns:

> Millions of people in our society suffer from poverty, malnutri-
> tion, inadequate housing, homelessness, debilitating health
> problems, and other serious needs. In the wider world, these
> problems are even more acute. The time and energy of those
> with resources must be shared freely with those who lack the
> vital necessities of life. Increasingly, governments are refusing
> to shoulder these responsibilities, so that the voluntary efforts
> of individual citizens become all the more important. How,

> then, is it conscionable for so many people to spend so much time within their own small groups attending to their own needs when the needs of others are so great? Can these groups be motivated to serve the wider community as well as their own members? (Wuthnow, 1994, 318)

I want to respond to Wuthnow's question, "can these groups be motivated" to look at social issues. I do not, of course, know for sure. However, some kinds of support are possible. We have already mentioned what seems like flatness in leadership. It would be valuable for the various SCC organizations and networks to provide leadership education that includes not only formation in the church's social teaching and in the prophetic tradition of scripture, but skills in social analysis, without which the implementation of social theory cannot fruitfully occur.

Second, this development would be helped greatly by the explicit support of the institutional church for the existence of SCCs and official encouragement to be actively apostolic. We who have worked on this research for over three years suspect that SCCs could be the church's best bet for implementing its social teaching. And third, the different publication houses that provide materials for SCCs could help communities focus more strongly on the social justice elements of the scriptures, and issue questions and discussion formats that assist communities in making connections with current situations.

In the several universities in which I have taught for 25 years in different parts of the country, the turnout for classes or workshops on anything to do with social justice has invariably been skimpy. Spirituality as a topic tends to draw a crowd. I will attempt to guess at the reason. In an affluent country such as ours, if the topic of social justice is not handled with some technical circumspection, middle-class people tend to feel guilty because they have more and some people have little or nothing. It takes some tactful and insightful approaches to the problem for people to understand the underlying systemic reason for deepening poverty in our country (and in the world). These approaches should be part of the formation of SCC leaders, and they deserve explicit attention in the various materials that are reproduced for them. This is beginning to happen. For example, in 1998, the Diocese of Oakland produced an excellent guide in both English and Spanish to help communities understand the religious need for social analysis, and to develop some skills *(Reading the Signs of the Times: Small Christian Community Material,* or, *Interpretando las Señales de Nuestro Tiempo: Material para Grupos Pequeños).*

Forming a More Biblical Catholic Identity

Except for ECCs, breaking open the Word is frequently the ritual centerpiece for SCC gatherings. And because of the sharing of scripture that is part of Eucharist, most of the observations that follow pertain to ECCs. I will suggest three areas for possible development in Catholic life: the forming of a scriptural Catholic identity; the *homiletic function* of the group process in SCCs; and the development of a new parish model.

Scripture and Catholic Identity

SCC Catholics are engaging their heritage (primarily scriptural rather than theological) in their small groups. Scripture is a dimension of their heritage that SCC activities make most accessible to members and which increasingly is informing their lives. There is little evidence that communities are fencing with their identity in doctrinal terms. Their Catholic identity and loyalty are clear, but their religious activity is focused on prayer and scripture. Some SCC members are aware of this shift in their sense of church identity: "And sure, in the majority it is a complete change, having their faith out of the gospel. Before, it was many traditions, right?" (H/L)

Data (especially from the interviews) suggest that Catholics' interaction with scriptural heritage in their SCCs is moving at least some of them toward a keener awareness of social issues (certainly that), and sometimes to social action (less often, that). If we succeed in encouraging communities to bring the social teaching of the church into the dialogue, the experience of mission is likely to increase. As I have already indicated, the materials prepared for SCCs could give more attention to social and systemic issues, as could the networks and organizations that nurture the communities.

Catholics have not traditionally been encouraged to read scripture on their own. Therefore, it is a novelty for many to discover for themselves the power of the Word in their lives. This development is fully consistent with the Vatican II document on divine revelation. The marginal life of SCCs may well be the pioneer territory where a more biblical Catholic identity is being tried on for size.

The Homiletic Dimension

The function of a homily is to help a community connect scriptural meaning with their lived experience and form a vivid dialogue between text and life to forge contemporary Christian praxis. The finest homilist in the world cannot regularly give a fifteen-minute sermon that is attentive to concrete human experience across a community's life.

The words of scripture, while precious and holy, do not fully become God's Word until the human situation has been addressed by them. God's Words to Moses involved such concrete situations as slavery, exodus, and freedom—likewise God's Words to David, Ezekiel, Mary, and Paul. We are addressed by God in the full details of our concrete experience. No small part of the power of an SCC is that it is a privileged place where the details of people's concrete experience are named and held up before the Word. This happens in the context of a very special kind of conversation between Word and world, one that needs a context like that of SCCs to happen with regularity and urgency in a community's life.

The Parish

If one could summarize the *magic* that attracts people to small Christian communities, it would be something like this:

> The SCC is a place of faith where we pray, sing, and explore scripture, and we know we are doing church. This is a place where we can bring our experience, our stories, and share them with people who are interested and supportive. Our conversation between faith and experience helps us create meanings out of which we are able to live. We have come to trust the process

that helps us make meaning, and to trust as well the meanings that emerge from our interaction. And these are processes and meanings we have come to trust.

The centerpiece is the process by which people actively dialogue their real experience with their faith, and thereby make meaning from which they choose to live. People who are not doing this in a small Christian community are far less likely to be doing it at all, for there is no ritual time and place made for it. The group process plays a very active, formative role in how people make their faith their own. Recall the clumsy expression from Jürgen Habermas cited earlier: *intersubjective communicative praxis.* In and through communication among people, a community's praxis is forged. It wells up out of the interpersonal dynamic.

The catechumenate is powerful because people are appropriating their faith aloud together with others. The community experience never replaces the personal processing and deciding that each must do, but it provides a context and a format that nourish the personal process (even as the personal faith nurtures the community's dynamics).

SCCs help us think that perhaps parishes in a future church will not imagine that they break the parish down into small Christian communities, but, like the early church, build the parish up out of small Christian communities. The National Alliance of Parishes Restructuring into Communities is perhaps a midway move. I have told Fr. Art Baranowski that I believe a major gift he has made to the U.S. church is to help us think of it with a different kind of imagination, one that retrieves the profoundly communal character of Catholic life.

If the small Christian communities are really to help reshape Catholic community at the parish level, there is a singular challenge that must be met. Some years ago my colleague, Michael Cowan, and I were invited to be consultants as a large diocese prepared for RENEW, and wanted RENEW communities to know that after RENEW a small Christian community was an option. Diocesan leaders recognized that the full support of pastors would make all the difference, if the efforts were to succeed. Several of the effective and respected pastors from the diocese were part of the consultation and named the challenge I want to note here. To become a real community, some genuine sense of responsibility must be located within the community. Then, a community will develop a spirit and an identity all its own. It will have character. The parish, these pastors said, must give them room to do that, and we, their pastors, must give up control to let that happen. But we have never been socialized to give up control, they said. I believe that is the challenge, to give them room to develop as something new in the church, and then to rethink what parish life might look like if it makes itself out of what emerges. There is, of course, some risk involved. The judgment made in the diocese supporting this direction was about the importance of keeping strong communication open between the communities themselves and between communities and the pastor, and that sounds right. It gives the Spirit room to do some new things with us. Given the data that show attachment to parish and to Catholic identity among SCC members, the risk appears worth taking.

Conclusion

What comes through clearly for many SCC members is that their relationship with the church is being reshaped. The fact of SCC membership is already an exercise of lay responsibility for faith that was far less evident in the preconciliar church. SCCs are moving scripture into a central place in their spirituality, for which the chance to relate scriptural meaning to lived experience through a group process is utterly crucial. Faith sharing activities also encourage SCC members to become more explicit about what being Catholic means to them. As a result of explicit attention to church issues, many members become more critical of the church but also practice a greater sense of charity toward it.

SCCs also seem to be both an expression and instrument of a greater acculturation of Catholicism to U.S. culture. In the process of acculturation, many Catholics have shifted their social location from ethnic enclave and working class to suburban and professional class. For most SCCs, these groups replace the extended family or ethnic enclave of an earlier time as a mechanism for transmitting and maintaining faith.

In a word, overall SCCs appear to be making a signal contri-bution to the movement of the U.S. Catholic Church into the third millennium.

Centers of Meaning

I would like to return to the text that appeared at the begin-ning of this book, a reflection offered by Craig Dykstra, Vice-President of the Religious Division of Lilly Endowment, Inc.

> Just getting through life involves having to figure a lot of things out.
>
> A lot of people are looking for help in figuring out what to do, in figuring out what is really going on in a situation, and in fig-uring out what our whole situation actually means.
>
> The help most people really want is a community of people in whose company they can do their own "figuring"—honestly, truthfully, and with a sense of integrity.
>
> What a gift it is if we are able to find a home place, a commu-nity of people who have really figured out how to go about fig-uring things out and thus live genuine lives!
>
> Developing that capacity more strongly is some of the most important work the Christian churches in our society have to do—now.
>
> Craig Dykstra
> *Initiatives in Religion*
> Winter 1998, 1–2, *passim*

I do not believe that members of Christian communities have everything figured out but that, in Dykstra's words, an SCC is "a community of people who have really figured out how to go about figuring things out and thus live genuine lives!" At the heart of the process of figuring things out is simply and profoundly a remarkable dialogue between articulated experience and articu-lated faith. Here is where that meaning is made in hearts, minds, and action. It is the transformative and emancipative creation of a Christian praxis.

As we have seen, members of small Christian communities attend to their internal needs, and are also learning to look beyond so that they can be centers of meaning not only for their immediate lived experience, but for the church and, in some limited but real ways, centers of meaning for the world through the church. It happened that way in the first three centuries. Why not now?

Appendix I
College and University Campus Communities
William V. D'Antonio

Introduction

Researchers studying religion in the United States and elsewhere have provided important information about the apparently dramatic falling off of religious practice among young adults: McNamara, 1992; Hoge et al., 1994; Fee et al., 1980–81; Roof and McKinney, 1987. We were aware from the beginning that young adults were not to be found in significant numbers among the main body of SCCs we knew anything about.[1] So we decided that one measure of religious activity among young Catholics might well be found in the presence of SCCs on college campuses across the country. To that end we sought and received from the National Office of Catholic Campus Ministers in Dayton a list of mailing addresses for 1,159 campus ministry offices. Presumably these were all the colleges and universities that had an office of campus ministry for Roman Catholics.

---

[1] For example, the percentage of Catholics in SCCs ages 18–29 ranged from 4 percent among GSCs to 9 percent among ECCs. Fully 81 percent of campus members fell into that category. And among those 30–39, there was a consistent average of 14 percent among the five other SCC types, while only 6 percent of the campus students were in that age category. Altogether then, less than one in five members of SCCs other than campus groups were in the age range between 18 and 39.

148

In Appendix II we provide a brief description of the sampling procedures we used to try to locate SCCs on college campuses. We drew a one-in-four sample from the list (289) and mailed a brief questionnaire designed to locate a contact person who could inform us of any SCC-like activity that might be taking place on campus. We received a total of 105 responses (a 36 percent response), 39 of which said they had one or more SCCs active in their campus ministry. We sent formal census forms to these 39, and 21 actually filled out and returned them to us. These forms indicated that there were at least 135 SCCs on these 21 campuses.

Based on the census count of 39 campuses reporting SCCs from the one-in-four sample, a cautious estimate would be that there are 160 campuses with some degree of SCC activity. And since campuses averaged between three and four SCCs per campus, we would expect as a conservative figure that there were between 540 and 560 SCCs on college campuses during the time of our study. *However,* when we carried out our saturation study of the eight dioceses, we located a total of 36 SCCs in these dioceses. Given that we found campus SCCs in six of the eight dioceses, we projected that there could be as many as 900 SCCs nationally on college campuses. It would seem safe to say then that there were somewhere between 540 and 900 SCCs on 160 to 250 college campuses during the time of our study. In terms of numbers of students and others who would be involved, given the average number of members reported as 27, we can say that there were somewhere between 14,580 students (the lower figure) and 24,300 students (the higher figure) active in campus SCCs during the time of our study.

The transient nature of campus life, the fact that SCC meetings were structured within terms and semesters, and that exams and graduations generally restricted the opportunity to develop any sense of community, the results we achieved with our census and motivation surveys, while limited, do provide a glimpse of a rich and rewarding communal Catholic life on some campuses. A summary overview of these findings follows.

A Profile of Campus SCCs

We begin with a table (Table 1) that summarizes basic information.

Appendix I / Table 1
Campus SCCs, a Demographic Profile

	Number or %
a. Average No. of Members per SCC	
Men	13
Women	14
Under age 18	4
b. Percentage of SCCs Meeting	
Weekly	81%
Biweekly	5
Monthly	10
Other	4
c. Percentage of SCCs Meeting in	
Member homes	14%
Parish building	29
Other (campus buildings)	57
d. Longevity of SCCs	
Less than One Year	29%
1–3	29
6–20	15
21+	19
e. Percentage of SCC Members at Age	
29 and under	83%
30–59	12
60 and older	5

(continued)

Appendix I / Table 1 *(continued)*

f. Percentage at Various Educational Levels	
Undergraduates	64%
Graduate students and graduates	33
g. Racial/ethnic Makeup of SCC	
African American	1%
Asian American	3
Hispanic/Latino	9
White non-Hispanic	86
h. Activities Engaged in at Every Meeting	
Prayer	95%
Spirituality	71
Faith sharing	57
Weekend Eucharist	57
Read and discuss scriptures	52
Theological reflection	29
Helping SCC members	24
Reaching out to larger community	24
Addressing structural issues	10

The first thing to note is the range in number of SCCs on campus. While some campuses like Yale fostered as many as 10–12 groups averaging 10–12 students each, a majority of campuses averaged two or three with closer to 30 members each as the norm (Table 1). Encouraging was the fact that men and women appeared in almost equal numbers on campus. It was also encouraging that the overwhelming percentage of campus groups met weekly, thus increasing the possibility of their developing close ties.

Table 1 also shows that the majority of student groups met in college buildings, dormitories, and Newman Centers. And almost six in ten had been in existence three years or less. We learned through the census reports and interviews that most campus groups included one or two nonstudent members, either faculty or other parishioners long associated with the campus parish. This gave the groups some stability over time.

We were surprised that one third of the groups had been in existence for six or more years, and that 17 percent of the members were 30 years old and older. And while graduate students made up significant numbers of some groups, these older members helped account for many of the college graduates listed among the members.

As we would expect, the great majority of all campus group members were white, with Hispanic/Latinos making up 9 percent of the membership. The latter figure of 9 percent is the highest percentage among all types of SCCs except for the charismatics (with 14 percent H/L) and the H/L groups themselves. Hispanic/Latinos are only now beginning to move into the college ranks in numbers that should eventually reflect more closely their proportion of the total U.S. population.

It is hard to interpret the fact that there is a smaller percentage of African Americans in campus SCCs than of Asian Americans. An effort to learn about recruitment of minorities as a part of SCC activity might be meaningful. Do African Americans find Newman and other Catholic centers on campus inviting places? The national statistics show about 4 percent of all Catholics to be African American; that would mean about 2.4 million Catholics. If at least 10 percent are going to college, where might we expect to find them?

Activities

Item "h" in Table 1 presents important information about the activities of SCCs. There are both similarities and differences in the activities of campus SCCs compared with other SCCs. Prayer is the common activity of all groups. Campus groups were the only ones to place spirituality second in terms of an activity engaged in at every meeting. In the final section on interviews, I will explore what they had in mind in giving such importance to spirituality.

Faith sharing was a major activity in most of the SCCs but only a small majority of campus groups engaged in it on a regular basis. The same was the case regarding reading and discussion of the scriptures. I suspect that the fact that these two activities were less central in campus groups could reflect the degree to which campus groups were or were not modeled closely on SCCs that have emerged from such national organizations as Buena Vista, National Alliance of Parishes Restructuring into Communities, or Post-RENEW and the North American Forum.

Apparently, many campus groups attended weekend Eucharist liturgy as a group, much more frequently than for any other SCC type except the ECCs.

The three items at the bottom of Table 1 refer to social justice issues. Here, students mirrored closely the GSCs in our study, with one in four concerning themselves regularly with the physical, psychological, or social well-being of their fellows, and with outreach toward the larger community in such works as helping in food kitchens, hospices, and the like. And given the circumstances of their lives on campus, it is not surprising that only one in ten addressed structural issues, such as national legislation, on a regular basis. To cite one example of this kind of discussion, I observed a gathering of a campus group on an evening just after the news announcement of the successful cloning of a sheep in England. This group devoted quite a bit of time to exploring the ethical implications of cloning within and across the areas of their academic specializations (medicine, law, physics, and humanities). Generally, however, their focus was on how to live the gospel in campus settings that were often distracting, if not in apparent conflict with gospel teachings.

Table 2 presents information from the motivations survey about individual members of campus SCCs.[2] We mailed some 331 questionnaires to individual student members of SCCs, and received 73 completed returns, a low 22 percent return rate. Thus, it is important to read the findings as only suggestive of what motivated students to join a campus SCC, and what it had meant to them. Given both the low return on the census and this low return, the student responses cannot be taken to necessarily represent campus SCCs, but only to suggest hypotheses for future testing.

---

[2]We were unable to distribute the attitudes survey to college groups because of calendar conflicts with the end of term and exams.

Appendix I / Table 2
Meaning of SCC Participation to Individual Members

1. Percentage of members saying SCC
   membership deeply satisfying   51%

2. Percentages indicating the factors
   most influential in their joining an SCC
       a. they were seeking a small group   41%
       b. the influence of friends   29
       c. the influence of a religious community 29
       d. the influence of a priest or nun   22
       e. the influence of a retreat experience   15

3. Percentage saying that SCC membership
       a. a new way of participating in
          parish life   51%
       b. a new way of being church for me   47
       c. the primary source of my spiritual
          nourishment   26
       d. led to a new sense of responsibility for
          parish and neighborhood   25
       e. led to a new sense of responsibility
          for civil society   18
       f. led me to be more involved in civil/
          political affairs   16
       g. led me to become more involved in
          pro-life and family issues   26
       h. led me to become more involved in
          parish activities   55

4. Attitudes toward pope/Vatican, percentage
       a. strengthened   37%
       b. weakened   —
       c. had no impact on   60

While half of the campus members said that SCC membership had been deeply satisfying, this was the lowest percentage
among all SCC types, where the more typical response ranged
between two out of three and 90 percent. They were similar to
other SCC members in saying that "seeking a small group" and the
"influence of friends" were the two most important factors in influencing their decision to join an SCC. Apparently, the influence of
priests and nuns and of a particular religious community played a
larger role in influencing them than was true for the other SCCs.

They were like the great majority of SCCs in the impact of
SCCs on their lives. A new way of participating in parish life and a
new way of being church were the two items they listed most frequently. And they reiterated the impact on parish life later when 55
percent said that the SCCs had led them to become more involved
in parish activities.

And while two out of three said that SCC membership had
had no impact on their attitude toward the pope or the Vatican, all
those who said it had had an impact said it had been positive in that
it had strengthened their attitude.

One dramatic way in which campus members differed from the
main body of young Catholics in the general U.S. population was in
Mass attendance. While only 26 percent of Catholics aged 18–39 in
our national sample said they went to Mass at least weekly, 90 percent of campus SCC Catholics said they did so. Of course, it may
well be that those Catholic students most likely to join SCCs were
the ones most likely to be regular Mass attenders. One of the ways
they would have learned of SCCs would have been from hearing an
announcement following Mass. We will explore the recruitment
process a bit more when we look at the interviews.

Perhaps the thing that stands out most clearly in Table 3 is that
no one item attracted more than a fourth of the students. Spiritual
nourishment, the most frequently noted reason for joining an SCC,
could result from any of the other items listed. None of the items is
exclusionary, but wanting to learn more about religion and God is
of a different dimension than joining to find a way to worship and
praise God. And, of course, seeking social support and new friends
can be seen as another way of talking about seeking a small community. The findings discussed in chapter three show that while the

Appendix I / Table 3
Most Important Personal Reasons for Joining an SCC

Spiritual nourishment	23%
Outreach to others in the larger community	18
Learn about religion and God	17
Social support, making new friends	17
Seeking a small community	15
Prayer, praise, worship	14

percentages differ, the same items appear to be the ones selected by other SCC Catholics, regardless of age.

For the most part, these young Catholics found in the SCCs what they had been looking for. The items most frequently mentioned by them as constituting the best part of their participation were: community/friendship (38 percent); sharing and exchanging (30 percent); learning about God (11 percent); and personal and spiritual growth (9 percent). These closely mirrored the responses of the members of the other SCCs.

Students were like other SCC members also in the kinds of things that proved most troublesome to them as members of SCCs.

Thirty percent cited "finding the time and meeting scheduling demands" as by far the most troublesome feature of SCC life. This was three times more frequently mentioned than the next two problems: the absence of members from meetings and the uncertain future of the particular group (mentioned by 11 percent), and finding it difficult to share faith experiences (also mentioned by 11 percent).

When they were asked what the main reasons were for continuing their membership in their SCC, one in four (26 percent) said that it was the feeling of fellowship—"like being part of a family," while one in five (20 percent) said "spiritual growth."

One of the notable pieces of data from Table 2 is that 37 percent said that their SCC membership strengthened their attitudes toward the pope and the Vatican, and none said that it weakened their attitude. This is remarkable in a somewhat turbulent time for the church's institutional life. But it is of a piece with the overall picture of SCC members as committed, faithful, churchgoing Catholics.

In Their Own Words: Letting Students Speak for Themselves

Our census data make it clear that college age young people and young adults do not constitute a very large part of the membership of SCCs. The nonpresence of many young people at church is no secret. We think it important, therefore, to understand why young people who do belong to SCCs believe it is helpful and important.

Further, our research has made it clear that the more educated Catholics are, the more likely they are to engage in critical reflection in faith areas as well as in all of the other areas of experience. Some of the conversation below indicates that young Catholics grapple with this and, basically, become comfortable with bringing their critical skills into faith life as well as the larger secular world.

The following quotations, summary statements, and paraphrases were taken from interviews and observations made on several college campuses in the East and Midwest. In letting the students speak for themselves, we tried to follow the findings reported in Tables 1–3 above, wherever possible. We began with the items listed in section "h" of Table 1, having to do with activities engaged in at every SCC meeting.

Here's how a student at a midwestern university reflected on his early participation in an SCC: "Church was not a big thing in my hometown; it was a very small part of my life. When I came to campus I heard about this SCC activity and wondered, what's that? So I checked it out and when I found that it was a small group talking about the gospel and life, I decided to join. And the first semester I thought it was really awesome. We had a format where we'd sit and we'd have a little bit of social time, read the gospel, talk about it, have some programming session, and at the end, prayer. It's every two weeks. It's like being on a retreat for a couple of hours every two weeks, to get away from it all, to vent frustration, to be there for each other." And another student added: "I found that it is wonderful to be able to talk with my peers and people I've gotten close to about God and not only about theological questions but also contemporary issues, like abortion. Things that are extremely important."

Another student saw the SCC as "a good support group. I was going through a lot of stuff second semester freshman year, trying to figure things out, and it was always good to know there was always somewhere I could go to talk about things that were bothering me. With people coming from different parts of the country, different backgrounds, different youth groups, kind of put a different spin on things."

On the significance of reading the scriptures at SCC meetings, one student noted: "I found that when we read the scripture ahead of time, when I hear it at Mass it makes so much more sense to me, and I understand it more and I want to listen to it more. And I'm less likely to phase out. And then I'm thinking, what does the priest think about it, and so I listen to his homily with more interest."

Another student focused on how the SCC allowed him and the others to talk about religion in a way they did not during the rest of the week. In the SCC "we talk about Catholic teachings, about American ways of thought, about the Vatican. For me it's a challenge to grow as a Catholic, to find out what I believe, what I'm supposed to believe...."

The sophomore year was particularly difficult for one student, who was having doubts, and hearing from smart people that it was "really not very smart to believe in God." But in her SCC she learned to be comfortable with doubt, that it was okay to question and to not always be sure. She concluded that "having that support and reassurance that it was okay to be questioning was really helpful to me...." When students, through their education, learn skills in critical reflection, it is helpful for them to know that critical reflection has a place in their faith life and church life as well. One young woman student from the Midwest observed: "I learned that just because somebody is Catholic doesn't mean that they believe what you believe. Not everybody who is Catholic believes the same things."

While that was clearly an important discovery among many SCC members, others felt that their SCCs provided a haven for serious discussion about matters religious and how they impact personally and socially. One student said because he knows of the commitments of his SCC he has been "a little more likely to start a conversation about outreach or to enter into a conversation about spirituality."

A student on the East Coast saw the SCCs as "part social group, part intellectual discussion group, where everyone has the common ground of Catholicism and then from there we discuss the main issues. But we really don't get much involved in outreach or service. We do that as a parish, we have a soup kitchen, but that's not part of the SCC activity as such."

Regarding outreach activities, one group leader in the Midwest made the point this way: "Community is not about taking care of each other; it's about reaching out. When we did our retreats last year, the theme of the retreat was service. Now a lot of students here do service, but we like to see them as a community go out and do a service project."

On Conflict and Disagreement

Students generally said that the structured nature of their gatherings mitigated against any real conflict. But they readily admitted that they were surprised to learn that just being Catholic was not enough to ensure consensus on every issue.

An interesting example of ideological conflict was recounted by a midwestern student who noted that one student was "just politically more conservative than the rest of the group. He identified himself as a Republican, whereas if you were to ask the others there about political affiliation, they are most likely to tell you 'Democrat,' and also likely to tell you 'liberal.'" Apparently, this conservative student dropped out temporarily because of RCIA obligations. But the group wanted him back because "he brings a different perspective to it (the group). And it really does help them to see things from his perspective...."

Another common problem had to do with the simple semantics of language. One student complained about students who were prone to the use of "we" in their monologues: "You know, 'we' should do this, Christ asks 'us' to do this. Well, who are you to say 'we'? Maybe you but not me."

On Values and Values Conflict

Many students acknowledged in one form or another the importance of the community as a place where they could feel free to express doubts about Catholicism. As one young woman said:

"Sometimes I felt guilty questioning [whether] what the Vatican says is right or whatever, but hearing how other people reacted and where they came from, where they stand on certain issues, really kind of comforts me, that I'm really not a bad person for disagreeing with one point or another. Just about everyone in our group questions one thing or another, but they still have strong values." In a related vein, another student said that the SCC has "showed me the human side of church."

One of the most startling responses about the impact of SCCs on their values came from a Yale senior who said: "Well, before I came to Yale the most important value was individual achievement. That's what gets you into Yale; that's what your parents insist on. Now, as I'm graduating from Yale, that is probably not that important to me. For me, particularly because of SCCs, partially because of St. Thomas More, partially because I'd been away from my family for so long, I think community that's developing that sense of belonging to a group, to a community, is much more important for me now than individual achievement. I now see that community is part of the solution to whatever problem you may have. You're on the right track if you're developing community."

Another student commented on the community impact of her SCC experience this way: "It (the SCC) emphasizes community, because when I see one of us at Mass, it reminds you of what we have every week; you're reminded that you're not just by yourself at church."

Students at Catholic colleges often mentioned the linkages between their particular SCC and the dormitory Masses they enjoyed. And they made comparisons with the impersonal nature of their home parishes: "Small faith communities make a difference because I come from a church that's enormous and the pastor doesn't know my name and will never know my name. My parents have switched back and forth between two parishes based on which one is more convenient to get to on Sunday morning. It's not a community. Here, I live in the smallest women's dorm on campus, so there are 75 people at Mass and I know 75 of them and I hug 75 of them at the sign of peace."

And another student: "When I think of graduating I'm scared. Every time I go home I'm kind of like, this just isn't the same. I'm actually thinking that I would like to join maybe a more charismatic church, maybe in hopes of having more interaction with the people around me." But another student took a slightly different view of the words *church* and *community:* "A couple of years ago our church back home burned down. And they're like that's okay, you still have your church, meaning the people together, supporting each other. So I think in essence the goal of Christian community is people together supporting each other."

Social Outreach

There was lots of discussion about the importance of outreach as an activity of SCCs, but the results were clearly mixed. One student from the Midwest acknowledged: "That was another one of those goals that we never really achieved. Because I'm really interested in social concerns and that's one of my main things that I do here, I tried to get people to go to the homeless shelter with me, but they don't want to do that."

The fact that young adults are still negotiating identity and intimacy needs may account in part for their attraction to the interpersonal dynamics of community life. But there is the larger context of American Catholics who, as a rule, do not instinctively connect their faith with public life.

The Spiritual Benefits of SCCs

A perhaps unexpected response came from a college professor who was active within an SCC on his campus. He said: "I think I've grown in my role of seeing Christ in our students more. I've been really impressed with the depth of their spirituality, and because of that I feel more encouraged to speak out about my own in my classes. In the past, I know I haven't been willing to do that."

A student commented that she felt that through the experience of the group "the Mass is a little more of a [spiritual] experience than it would have been. It's not enough to just be at a Catholic school. Groups like this make it more special; it's not enough to just go to Mass on Sunday and not think about it for the rest of the week."

One student looked back on his SCC experience with the following thoughts: "The SCC forces you to name your faith, like that's such a huge part of your spiritual journey and your spirituality is naming what's going on in your life. We had a retreat—and there were moments that were like comfortable silence, but most of the time we were just talking. And I thought it was really a moving experience because we were talking about how we had gone through our journey at [the] university and our spirituality had changed over our journey and our lives had changed. It was just really neat to see all of us have to name that, have to go through and discuss that and put a label on it, and it was a very moving experience for all of us. This was a moment of realization, of where we were, where we were going."

A final thought on spirituality, which is probably close to the reality of most human experience: "I know I've grown spiritually, but I don't know if it's the community or a lot of other outside factors; they're involved too. So I think it's probably a combination."

Summary

As we have already stated, our data on campus SCCs are somewhat limited, but ample enough to sense general configurations that are trustworthy. The data from our limited findings based on the census, the motivations survey, and the few interviews we were able to complete suggest that students who participate in campus SCCs are very active Catholics, are genuinely nourished spiritually, and said that SCC activity led them to be more active in campus parish life than they otherwise would have been.

Appendix II
Research Methodology—A Narrative
William V. D'Antonio

Introduction

Our study of small Christian communities (SCCs) was carried out in several stages over three years, beginning with a planning grant in 1995, and extending through 1998. The 1995 census that we conducted allowed us to identify six distinct types of small Christian communities for our study (which was updated as additional data became available). This census also provided demographic profiles that made it possible to compare and contrast the six types.

We then sampled the SCC types with two surveys. First, a motivations survey explored the reasons that individuals joined an SCC, as well as the outcomes of their participation. Second, an attitudes survey explored values, beliefs, attitudes, and behaviors of SCC members.

We secured the services of the Research Center at the University of Maryland to conduct a survey of the general Roman Catholic population in the United States. We also used the attitudes survey in this national random sample of the U.S. Catholic population, enabling us to compare and contrast SCC members with the general Catholic population.

We concluded our data gathering with participant observation of SCC gatherings and interviews with SCC members in the several parts of the country.

Making Contact with Communities

We began this study with a considerable amount of knowledge about sources that were helping to stimulate the growth of SCCs in the Catholic Church in the United States. The leaders of the major SCC movements had already promised us their support, and the general atmosphere was one of optimism about and enthusiasm for the study. From the beginning we were in contact with the following organizations most active in encouraging the development of SCCs:

- Buena Vista (BV), Arvada, Colo.

- Eucharist Centered Communities (ECC; formerly called Intentional Eucharistic Communities), Washington, D.C.

- International Office of RENEW, Plainfield, N.J.

- Marianist Lay Network of North America, Dayton, Ohio

- Mexican American Cultural Center, San Antonio, Tex.

- Ministry Center for Catholic Community, Seattle, Wash.

- National Alliance of Parishes Restructuring into Communities (NAPRC), Troy, Mich.

- North American Forum for Small Christian Communities (NAFSCC), Louisville, Ky.

- Pastoral Office for Small Christian Communities, Archdiocese of Hartford, Conn.

- Secretariat for Hispanic Affairs, National Conference of Catholic Bishops (NCCB), United States Catholic Conference (USCC), Washington, D.C.

Also of importance in helping us frame our thinking about SCCs was J. Vandenakker's 1994 book, *Small Christian Communities and the Parish*, an ecclesiological analysis of the experience of SCCs in North America. In addition to the organizations we already knew about, Vandenakker identified the St. Boniface Parish in Pembroke

Pines, Florida, as fostering a particular form of SCC called the Cell System. He also identified as an SCC type the movement called SINE (Systematic Integral New Evangelization), originating in Mexico, under the leadership of Rev. Alfonso Navarro. SINE is spreading slowly through the Southwest and other parts of the United States.

Following the Buena Vista Convocation in the Bon Secours Retreat House, just outside Baltimore, Maryland, January 26–29, 1995, we met with the leaders of organizations and movements connected in any way with SCCs (of which we were aware at that time). Included in the meeting were the teams of theologians and social scientists who became the key associates and consultants to the study.

Although none of the organizations listed above had carried out a systematic survey of SCCs, they were eager to have us do so and provided us with a general sense of the nature of the SCCs they were trying to foster and of the activities in which SCCs were expected to engage. This information helped us formulate the census questionnaire, which we then pretested, revised, and used in the initial phase of the research.

To help us carry out a census that would fairly represent the various types of SCCs, the movement leaders provided us background information about their organizations, rough estimates of the number of persons active within their movements, and lists of the contact persons, parishes, and dioceses active within their movements.

Before we describe our research procedures, sampling methods, and the like, we begin with a brief description of the groups and organizations that have been most responsible for the emergence and growth of the SCC movement in the United States, since these were so central to our efforts to locate and contact SCCs in this country.

National Alliance of Parishes Restructuring into Communities (NAPRC). The National Alliance of Parishes Restructuring into Communities (NAPRC) began with the work of a Michigan priest, Fr. Arthur Baranowski, who had been involved in organizing SCCs since the 1970s, and had spent one year in the national RENEW office. A 1989 *National Catholic Reporter* (NCR) article described Father Baranowski as "the only parish priest with long-term experience with small Catholic communities outside the charismatic movement." In *Creating Small Faith Communities* (1988), Father Baranowski explained that the goal of the NAPRC was to change the parish structure (to restructure it) because "the parish as presently structured no longer brings us together to experience well what makes us Catholic Christians."

Small Christian communities lay at the core of this restructuring of the parish. To this end, Baranowski has tirelessly toured the country giving workshops and promoting SCCs.

The NAPRC is a loosely organized collectivity. It has a board of directors with 11 members (nine of whom were priests), and a nine-person operations team. All are volunteers except a part-time national coordinator. The NAPRC kept a file on all correspondence and activity, dividing its contents into nine categories. We examined these categories in an attempt to understand better the extent of the NAPRC's activity.

Father Baranowski and his team (every member of the board plus four trained presenters) had given workshops for pastors and parish members from some 700 parishes in roughly 100 dioceses in the United States, beginning in 1989. The NAPRC office estimated that about 600 parishes were in the process of restructuring into SCCs. We mailed questionnaires to 220 people (a one-in-three sample) who had attended one or more of the NAPRC workshops. The returns showed that about 60 percent had formed or were forming SCCs within their parish. It was clear that the NAPRC was an important part of the SCC movement.

Buena Vista. Buena Vista (BV) came into being in 1987 when a married couple (Mike and Barbara Howard), who had been active in their diocesan RENEW program and in SCCs for almost 17 years, decided to convene a gathering of interested persons in Buena Vista, Colorado. Out of that gathering came an organization and the agreement to communicate by means of a bimonthly newsletter. By 1995, there were about 450 dues-paying members—including laity, priests, religious, and some parishes—in small study groups located in ten regions throughout the country.

To stimulate interest, Buena Vista sponsored annual and regional convocations. In the words of the Buena Vista mission statement, the focus of SCC activity was "on prayer, sharing, listening, learning, and discerning."

We carried out two preliminary studies of the BV membership: (1) a one-in-four sampling of the national membership to ascertain participation in SCCs; and (2) a survey of the people who attended the BV conference in Bon Secours, Maryland, in January 1995, to learn about the extent of their participation in SCCs and the relationship of BV to their participation. An examination of the results showed that BV did indeed foster the development and nourishment of SCCs through its conferences and through the efforts of its members and national officers. Vandenakker had identified BV as fitting the theological criteria for an SCC, and our preliminary findings reaffirmed its place in this study.

North American Forum for Small Christian Communities. Brochures for the North American Forum for Small Christian Communities (NAFSCC) describe it as "a membership organization for diocesan personnel involved in the ministry of Small Christian Communities." These materials trace the origin of the NAFSCC back to 1984, when diocesan and national RENEW staff met to discuss continuing to support the small groups that had been formed in parishes during the formal phase of RENEW. "The first gathering was called with the purpose of differentiating between existing national groups, legitimating the experience of small communities and giving direction to the movement." Here, again, we saw the influence of RENEW in the SCC experience. By 1995, the NAFSCC had grown into a national organization with a membership of 50 dioceses. Each diocesan chancery office provided the dues for four persons annually, with at least one holding the office of SCC director.

We sent a questionnaire to each of the 50 NAFSCC diocesan contacts, inquiring about SCC activity in each of their dioceses. The data we received from this questionnaire, a review of NAFSCC literature, and conversations with NAFSCC leaders confirmed the NAFSCC's important role in the U.S. SCC movement. Again, Vandenakker had included the NAFSCC as an SCC type, and we have included it in our research.

RENEW. First, RENEW is clearly one of the most important reasons for the spread of SCCs, but is itself not one of the six SCCs in the study. We explain why below, but nevertheless appreciate the importance of including RENEW in this section as the chief stimulant in the growth of SCCs.

In 1976, Bishop Peter Gerety of Newark, N.J., developed the idea of parish renewal as a way to bring alive the spirit of Vatican II. Under the leadership of Frs. Thomas A. Kleisler and Thomas P. Ivory, the RENEW movement was carefully developed and then formally launched in the Newark Diocese between 1978 and 1980. The RENEW idea was that people were being asked not to reform or restore or revolutionize their faith, only to renew it.

The idea caught on quickly and well. By 1995, RENEW had been activated in some 120 dioceses within the United States, and had been launched in more than 100 dioceses outside the country. By the time we completed the data-gathering stage of our study, an additional 12 dioceses had joined the RENEW movement.

James Kelly, a Fordham University sociologist, carried out an evaluation study of RENEW in 1986 and estimated that in the Newark Diocese alone some 40,000 Catholics had participated in RENEW. Kelly also estimated that approximately 310,000 Catholics had participated in some or all of RENEW in the several dioceses that were included in his research. From numbers offered by him and statistics provided by the international RENEW office in New Jersey, it seemed reasonable to estimate that RENEW had attracted 3 million or so Catholics to its small groups since its inception in 1980.

There are 175 regular dioceses and roughly 20,000 parishes listed in the Kenedy Directory (1993). Given that 120 dioceses had experienced RENEW by 1995, we estimated that RENEW had been part of the parish life of at least 10,000 parishes in the 15 years since the program had spread out from Newark.

The operational directors of RENEW made it clear that they saw RENEW more as a stimulant for the development of SCCs than as the direct creator of SCCs. This idea of RENEW as a stimulant or forerunner to the creation of SCCs was less clear to many of the laity who participated in RENEW, according to those at the meeting most familiar with RENEW. Apparently, many laity saw themselves as participating in SCCs as part of the RENEW experience.

It seemed clear that the limitation on RENEW as an SCC was that the RENEW groups within parishes met for six-week periods twice a year over a span of three years when RENEW formally ended. Kelly had concluded from his evaluation of RENEW that the most important effect of RENEW was that it gave parishioners an opportunity to experience prayer and the reading and discussion of scripture in the context of small faith-sharing groups.

It was obvious from the data and the meeting discussion that RENEW had been an important factor in the broad-based move to establish SCCs within parishes. To encourage that movement further, the international office of RENEW had established a department that provided assistance for ongoing SCC development. To that end, the leaders had created a series of pamphlets and booklets for leadership development in a small-community context and had published the book titled *Small Christian Communities: A Vision of Hope*.

The leaders of RENEW made manifest their intention to play a major role in this new stage of the movement, called Beyond RENEW. By 1995, 53 dioceses had each set up an office for small Christian communities in collaboration with the Beyond RENEW effort. To help us with our study, the RENEW office provided the names of the contact persons in those dioceses.

Vandenakker had identified the parish RENEW groups as SCCs; however, we decided not to include in our study groups that were actively participating in parish RENEW. We did gather as much information as we could from all sources about RENEW but have limited our study to the groups that formed as part of Beyond RENEW.

Although these organizational contacts provided us with the basic information we needed, we also ran notices of the research in several periodical publications that provided additional contacts: the *National Catholic Reporter* (NCR) and the *Call to Action Newsletter*, *Pace*, and *Sojourners*.

Christian Life Communities. During the early planning phase, we became aware that the Jesuit Sodality Movement that had been in existence since the time of Ignatius was being transformed in

the United States into the Christian Life Communities movement (CLC). Inspired by the documents of Vatican II, the CLC
movement gradually began to spread. Its 1995 directory identified 64 CLCs in the United States. Our contact with their leaders
and reading of their literature indicated that they saw themselves
as SCCs, and the information available about them indicated
they fit the criteria, so we included the CLCs in our study. Central to their own mission was a preferential option for the poor.
They hold both regional and national conventions, and have
been active in promoting the CLC idea in Jesuit high schools and
colleges. Vandenakker did not list CLCs as an SCC, but we found
that they fulfilled the criteria, and so they are included as a subtype of the GSC.

The SCC Typology: Five Major Categories

Based upon similarities indicated in the census survey, we for-
mulated the following typology, used throughout the research that
followed.

Type One: GSC, General (Type) of Small Community

We call the largest SCC type General Small Communities
(GSC). These communities are about 65 percent of those located in
our research. This type includes communities that are part of or
related to Buena Vista; National Alliance of Parishes Restructuring
into Communities; North American Forum for Small Christian
Communities; Christian Life Communities; Beyond or Post-
RENEW; and all those parish-connected groups that may have
been established because of laity, religious, or clergy.

Type Two: H/L, Hispanic/Latino Communities

The H/L communities constitute about 20 percent of those
located in our study, and they are a fast growing type of small Christian community.
We relied on several sources to obtain information about ministry to the growing numbers of Hispanics/Latinos in the United

States. In addition to the Secretariat for Hispanic Affairs at the National Conference of Catholic Bishops/United States Catholic Conference (NCCB/USCC), we were assisted by the Mexican American Cultural Center, and by several priests and women religious, including Fr. José Marins (a Brazilian priest active in SCC workshops), Sr. Ninfa Garza, and Edgard Beltran.

We mailed two sets of questionnaires to Latino SCC leaders: one to a list we received from the Mexican American Cultural Center and one to a list provided by Father Marins. The responses indicated that the Latino SCCs are similar to other SCCs, that is, similar in structure, frequency of meetings, and group activities. Two-thirds of the respondents said that they saw absolutely no difference between Base Ecclesial Communities (BEC)—common in some areas of the United States—and SCCs. Further, nearly 90 percent said that many, most, or all of the SCCs in their diocese were "essentially the same as Base Ecclesial Communities."

The information from our questionnaires, information provided by the organizations named above, and conversations with a variety of other Latino SCC leaders allowed us to identify the Latino small Christian communities as well within the boundaries of this study. Vandenakker himself had focused most of his attention on the Base Ecclesial Communities. To ensure stability and longevity, he emphasized the importance of their being institutionally linked to parish structures. This was certainly the intent of the NCCB in the specially constructed document that was approved for the Hispanic ministry in January 1996.

From the beginning, we considered Hispanic/Latino SCCs as a separate type because of the special effort being directed to the Latino Catholic population in the United States and because they were known to have several distinctive demographic characteristics: first and second generation in the United States; younger age cohorts than the rest of the Catholic population (and much lower formal education than the rest of the Catholic population); and because these communities are almost entirely composed of Hispanic Catholics (very little ethnic diversity).

Type Three: Chr, Charismatic Prayer Groups/Communities

The charismatic communities constitute about 12 percent of the communities located in our study.

One of the respondents to our notice in the *National Catholic Reporter* was Walter Matthews, executive director of Chariscenter, U.S.A., the executive office of the Catholic Charismatic Renewal of the U.S., Inc. Matthews pointed out that the 5,141 prayer groups then a part of Chariscenter saw themselves as SCCs, and he sent a body of literature describing the history, mission, and current activities of the movement. After meeting with him and carefully examining the information provided, we decided that the charismatic prayer groups did indeed qualify as SCCs; hence, we included them in our study. Their 1992 and 1997 directories provided more complete information about SCCs than was provided by any other national organization. As will become apparent in the following sections, these directories were vital in helping us in our sampling procedures.

Together these three groups (GSC, Chr, and H/L) constitute 97 percent of the communities in our study. A number of different kinds of groups comprise the remaining 3 percent, of which we focus upon two: those with Call to Action connections and Eucharist Centered Communities.

We inserted a notice in the *National Catholic Reporter,* in the *Call to Action Newsletter,* in *Pace,* and in *Sojourners,* asking people to notify us if they belonged to a group that might be an SCC not affiliated with any of the known national organizations. About 100 responses informed us of the existence of SCCs of varying sizes and focuses. In each case, we followed up by inviting the respondent to fill out a questionnaire. A significant minority were SCCs that had developed on their own or with the encouragement of a priest, a woman religious, or other parish leader. Some were clearly related to the organizations listed above.

A significant number, however, were identified as Eucharist centered, and for the first time we became aware of groups that identified with the national Call to Action (CTA) organization. The latter led us to the CTA Directory, an analysis of which led us to delineate CTA SCCs as another type.

Type Four: CTA, Call to Action

The 1995 and 1996 CTA directories provided descriptions of more than 100 groups that identified themselves as small Christian communities. Most if not all of the groups in the CTA directories had come into being independent of the national CTA organization. Each listed itself voluntarily to let others know of its existence, vision, and mission. In the course of this study, groups have been organizing that consciously identify themselves as CTA regional or state associations. Letters of inquiry and follow-up census questionnaires helped build a type that comprised 94 confirmed SCCs.

As is made evident in the body of our study, the CTA communities are similar in demographics, belief, attitudes, and behavior to the ECCs (described below); the characteristic that distinguishes them is simply whether they did or did not build their community around celebration of the Eucharist. Thus, groups that were listed in the directories and responded to the census questionnaire were placed in the CTA category if they did not include celebration of the Eucharist in their gatherings; if they did, they were placed in the ECC type.

Type Five: ECC, Eucharist Centered Communities

When we began our study, we were aware of 15 small communities that identified themselves as Intentional Eucharistic Communities (IECs), which appear as Eucharist Centered Communities in our study (ECCs). An important early consideration was whether all 15 ECCs that were part of the 1991 IEC Conversation (held in Washington, D.C.) still were active. The data derived from the 1991 gathering (histories, mission statements, structures, importance of outreach, and the fact that celebration of the Eucharist was a central part of their worship) encouraged us to include them in the study. During the three-year study, we found and renamed a total of 70 Eucharist Centered Communities (ECCs) as we identify them in this study.

Additional SCC Experiences

While the following groups do not receive specific attention in the body of this text, they are sufficiently active at least to name them.

College Campus Communities

Early on, we realized that the SCCs that were a part of the organizations and movements spelled out above were largely lacking in young people, that is, those between 18 and 35. The National Campus Ministry Office in Dayton University provided us with 1,159 mailing labels of Catholic campus ministry offices on the campuses of Catholic and other private and public colleges and universities in the United States. (There are about 3,000 colleges and universities in the United States, including two- and four-year colleges.) The labels included just about all the Catholic colleges and probably most of the colleges with any significant number of Catholic students enrolled.

We drew a one-in-four random sample from the labels, mailed letters to ensure that the labels reflected active campus offices, and inquired if the campuses had any SCCs. We received 105 responses, a 36 percent return rate. Of the 105 returns, 39 reported that they had one or more SCCs active on the campus. In the ensuing census questionnaire mailing, only 21 of the 39 returned questionnaires. The data from the returned questionnaires were sufficiently in line with our criteria that we felt secure in designating these groups as SCCs and including them in our study. Despite the transiency of the campus groups occasioned by graduation, we felt it important to have some idea of SCC campus activity. Although we had excellent contacts and feedback from several schools, the overall quality and quantity and representativeness of the data were sufficiently marginal that we did not include them in the body of the report. A special summary of major findings about campus communities is provided in Appendix I.

St. Boniface Cell System

We wrote to Fr. Michael Eivers, the pastor of St. Boniface Parish in Pembroke Pines, Florida, and the developer of the Cell System, in an effort to build on what we had already learned about the St. Boniface Cell System from Vandenakker's analysis (1994). Father Eivers learned about the method of "celling," that is, creating within a parish small groups of roughly 12 persons each, from the Korean Assemblies of God Pastor Paul Yonggi Cho (*Successful Home Cell Groups*, [South Plainfield, N.J.: Bridge Publishing Company, 1981]). Pastor Cho had a church of 500,000 members that he subdivided into 50,000 cells, in Seoul, South Korea. The church of St. Boniface was reported to have more than 600 members involved in some 50 cell groups, averaging 10 to 12 members each. To foster the growth of the cell system, Father Eivers sponsored annual conferences at St. Boniface to explain the system to interested pastors and pastoral workers.

The main thrust of the cell groups was evangelization, but Father Eivers also stressed the role of the cells as *mediating communities*. By this he meant that the cells helped mediate the experience of church in a more personal way to the individuals who participated in them than was possible in the larger parish congregation. Father Eivers listed the seven purposes of cell groups:

1. To grow in intimacy with the Lord
2. To grow in love of one another
3. To share Jesus with others
4. To minister in the Body
5. To give and receive support
6. To raise up new leaders
7. To deepen our Catholic identity

At the time of our correspondence, Father Eivers had just moved to a new pastorate at St. Edward's, also in Pembroke Pines. He expressed the hope that he would soon have a cell system in place there.

The materials provided by Father Eivers and others indicated that the SCC cell-system style had been adopted by people in at least several other parishes in the country as well as in Europe; we were unable to obtain a list of the parishes. We included St. Boniface parish in our census, and discovered that there were only 22 cells active in late fall 1995. It appeared that the change in pastors was having an impact on the system.

The most distinctive feature of these cells was that some were racially and ethnically integrated, others were wholly white, Jamaican, or Latino. Because we were not able to procure the names of other parishes that had a developed cell system, we decided not to include the cell system in our study even though the census data indicated that it met the criteria for an SCC type.

Communities Related to Religious Orders

A member of the Lay Marianist Network explored whether Catholic religious orders in the United States were involved in SCCs in a formal way. The director placed several ads in the *National Catholic Reporter*, contacted the Leadership Conference of Women Religious (LCWR), the Conference of Major Superiors of Men's Orders (CMSM), and the national offices of several religious orders. These contacts turned up very few additional SCCs. We also learned that the great majority of Lay Marianist groups met only a few times a year, not frequently enough to engage in outreach activities, or to dialogue, carry on faith-sharing activities, and seek to understand the scriptures for their daily lives.

Since our study was initiated, a new organization has come into existence, *Associates*, which networks religious orders with associate communities and also networks the associate communities themselves. The national coordinator of associates, Jean Sonnenberg, indicates a membership of about 14,500, and believes that these communities share many of the characteristics of SCCs.

Teams of Our Lady

We also learned early on of an international organization, Teams of Our Lady, chartered by the pope in 1947. In the United States at the time of the study, there were some 5,000 teams, made up of married couples, who met once a month for prayer, scripture reading, faith sharing, and dinner. The national secretariat was reluctant to make available to us the mailing lists of the members; an overview of their mission statement and conversation with members showed that they did not think of themselves as part of the SCC movement, and they were not mentioned by Vandenakker in his book. They are not included as a formal group in this study.

Locating and Mapping the SCCs by Regions and Dioceses

One of the initial goals of our study was to map the SCC movement across the country. We wanted to know what parts of the country exhibited the most extensive and intensive SCC activity. And whether different SCC types exhibited different patterns of activity.

Given the dynamic nature of the movement, the various sponsors of SCC activity, the range of SCC types, and the realization that SCCs had emerged out of national and local as well as personal initiatives, we decided to map SCCs nationally within a diocesan framework.

The charismatic prayer groups were easy to map because they were already arranged by diocese in their directory, published every five years. Our initial efforts revealed that SCC activity had reached all regions of the country. The National Conference of Catholic Bishops has divided the United States into 13 regions, within which it has placed the 175 Catholic dioceses. To simplify our census mapping and subsequent sampling procedures, we divided the dioceses into eight regions. Using a table of random numbers, we drew two samples, each containing one diocese from each region. Having assured ourselves that they were both representative of the national population of Catholics, we selected the first for use in the study. Table 1 compares the percentage of Catholics within the diocese sampled with the percentage of Catholics in the region as a whole.

According to the official Kenedy Directory, from which these figures were taken, in 1993 Catholics totaled 59,220,723, 23 percent of the U.S. population of 256,042,585. Overall, the dioceses we sampled were 22.3 percent Catholic; the percentage of Catholics in the eight regions was 22.8 percent. Thus, overall, our sample reflects the eight regions within one-half of 1 percent.

In three of the regions the diocese under study had a lower percentage of Catholics than the region as a whole; in one diocese (Las Cruces) the Catholic population exceeded the regional average by a significant percentage. Although the Charlotte Catholic population was only 3 percent of the total, the region as a whole was 9 percent Catholic, suggesting that our sample might under-represent Catholics in the region. So, the overall sample is representative, but there are some variances.

Appendix II / Table 1
Percentage of Catholics Sampled

Diocese/Region	Diocese	Region
Manchester/New England	29%	39%
Pittsburgh/Mid-Atlantic	40	38
Charlotte/South-Atlantic	3	9
Ft. Worth/West South Central	8	16
Youngstown/Midwest	23	24
Dubuque/West Central	25	21
Las Cruces/Mountain	31	15
Fresno/Pacific	19	16
average	22.3%	22.8%

Catholics in the eight dioceses of the study totaled 2,371,282, or 4 percent (1/25th) of the U.S. Catholic total. Thus, our estimate of the number of SCCs for the types in which the national number is not known will be based on extrapolations from these eight dioceses. In essence, where we estimate the total based on sampling within regions, we will multiply the sample number by 25 to reach a national estimate.

We found SCCs in all eight regions of the country, but only the charismatics had groups within every diocese. In cases where we did not find SCCs within one of the eight dioceses in our study, we sampled within the region to keep the sample as representative as possible.

Completing the Census

Preliminary findings indicated that the leaders of Beyond RENEW, the NAFSCC, BV, and the NAPRC had worked closely with one another. Moreover, there were many SCCs that said they were mixtures of these types. And the early responses to questionnaires supported the position that these SCCs could all be grouped together as one master type. Because the responses of the CLCs seemed to fit this larger pattern, they were also included in this one master SCC, which we have called General Small Communities

(GSCs). Our GSC type includes representative samples of the several groups, coded so that we can separate out the subtypes if it should be found desirable to do so.

Carrying out the census proved to be a multistage process, as suggested by the discussion above. We knew the universe of the population of three of the six SCC master types: Call to Action; charismatic prayer groups; and Eucharist Centered Communities.

A. The CTA and ECC Census. We decided that we would try to include all known CTA and ECC SCCs in our study, so we mailed questionnaires to all known contacts. We received 94 CTA and 70 ECC completed returns. Because these returns constitute all the known ECCs, and 90 percent of the known CTAs, we know the findings reflect accurately these two SCC types.

B. The Charismatic Prayer Groups Census. The 1992 Directory of Charismatic Prayer Groups listed 5,141 prayer groups in the United States. Using a random sample stratified by region, we mailed 298 census questionnaires, and received 99 completed forms, a 33 percent response rate. Given the broad national distribution of the responses, we adjudged these an adequate representative sample.

C. The GSC Census (including Buena Vista, the NAPRC, the NAFSCC, Post-RENEW, CLC, and others). We had the mailing list of the 451 members of Buena Vista, so in a sense knew the universe of members. But we did not know how many were actively involved with SCCs. We did a one-in-three sample and received 96 completed forms, a 62 percent return.

We had the list of workshop participants of Baranowski's National Alliance, with preliminary findings suggesting that about 60 percent were active in SCCs. Again, we did a one-in-four sample (136), and received 41 completed forms. Although this represented only a 30 percent return, we noted that on many of the BV, NAF, and other returns, people included the NAPRC as being one of the sources for their structure and functioning. We found no other indication of bias or reason for nonresponse, and concluded that the return rate was adequate for our purposes.

The North American Forum and Post-RENEW lists revealed significant overlap in dioceses and leadership. After merging the lists, we found 55 dioceses in which one or both organizations were active.

Through their contacts we were able to build a list of parishes in which there were active SCCs. We then had to proceed to the parish level to learn the number and contact persons for their SCCs. Within parishes the number of SCCs ranged from one or two to as many as 57. (To provide some idea of the dynamics of this movement, we learned in early 1998 that the parish with 57 SCCs in 1995 counted 72 active groups in early 1998.) Again, using stratified random sampling, we mailed 409 census questionnaires and received 206 responses, a 50 percent return rate. The representation reflected the eight regions into which the country was divided for sampling purposes. Some groups noted their ties to Buena Vista and the NAPRC.

We followed the same procedures with the Jesuit Christian Life Communities (nine groups), the groups that our notices in various Catholic periodicals brought to our attention (88 groups), and with several other lists at our disposal. The census was completed with a saturation survey of the eight dioceses selected for our sampling. Based on the earlier findings, we decided to seek SCCs within the dioceses that might not be connected with any of the national organizations. Using the Kenedy Catholic Directory (1993), we drew random samples of parishes within each of the eight dioceses and made personal telephone calls to the pastors. In addition to the SCCs about which we already knew, these contacts produced lists of SCCs that were not related to any of the above, and constituted the final group (75) in our general GSC type. There were also seven census questionnaires whose relationship to the above organizations was not clear; they were also placed in the GSC type.

D. The Hispanic/Latino Census. Multiple contacts with Latino offices and diocesan leaders provided us with about 150 contacts nationally. These gradually yielded a sample of some 500 groups in 26 dioceses. Again, a one-in-four sample across dioceses and regions yielded 125 completed census forms. Saturation samples within the eight dioceses selected for the study added few new groups to those about which we already knew.

Estimating the Number of SCCs in the United States by Type

In Table 2, we provide the estimates of SCCs within each diocese by type. In some dioceses, we received data that provided us

Appendix II / Table 2
Estimated Number of SCCs by Type and Diocese

Region/diocese	GSC	Chr	CTA	ECC	H/L
Manchester/					
New England	35	15	1	—	—
Pittsburgh/					
Mid-Atlantic	248	44	1	—	—
Charlotte/					
South-Atlantic	140	24	1	—	35
Ft. Worth/					
West					
South Central	132	16	1	—	50
Youngstown/					
Midwest	153	13	—	—	3
Dubuque/					
West Central	142	19	2	—	2
Las Cruces/					
Mountain					
(low)	55	26	—	—	(low) 81
(high	115				(high) 165
Pacific-Fresno	16	19	—	—	44
Totals (low)	921	176	6	—	215
(high)	981				299

with the best estimate of SCCs throughout all the parishes in the diocese. In other cases, there was no central source that could confirm actual numbers. In those cases, we began by seeking BV, NAF, Post-RENEW, NAPRC, and CLC activity within each diocese. We then completed a random sample of parishes within the diocese under study. We telephoned each parish, seeking information from the pastor and/or the persons in charge of SCC activity. After completing the sampling and deducting any cases that had appeared through one of the national SCC organizations, we extrapolated from the number found through sampling to the diocesan level based on whether the sample was a one-in-three, four, or other. Sampling was used to obtain the GSC data in Manchester, Pittsburgh, Youngstown, Las Cruces, and Fresno.

Appendix II / Table 3
Estimated SCCs in United States by Type

SCC Type	Sample N	United States* N
GSC	921 (low)	23,025
	981 (high)	24,525
CTA	6	94 (CTA directory)
ECC	0	70 (by census)
Chr	176	4,400
	204	5,141 (by 1992 directory
	184	4,860 (by 1997 directory)
H/L	215 (low)	5,375
	299 (high)	7,475

*To arrive at the national figure, we multiplied the number found within the particular diocese by 25, because the dioceses represented 4 percent of the national Catholic total.

Sampling was not used in the case of Chrs because in each diocese we were able to obtain local data from the diocesan liaison specifying the totals.

Because we knew the total number of CTAs by reason of having their directory, we merely noted the number of CTAs that were found in the particular dioceses. There were no ECCs in any of the eight dioceses under study.

In the case of Las Cruces, the diocese had begun a huge RENEW 2000 SCC program, and we decided to list the number of SCCs for Hispanics and GSCs excluding the RENEW 2000 program (the low figure) and the number including the program (the high figure).

Table 3 presents the estimates for the United States as a whole. The data from the charismatic prayer groups were especially helpful in encouraging us to believe that our estimates provide good ball-park figures. Note that our 1997 survey of the eight dioceses produced a count of 176 charismatic prayer groups. The 1997 directory listed 184 prayer groups in those eight dioceses. Thus, our diocesan sample was within 5 percent of their official count. However, our national estimate of 4,400 Chr groups, based on the information from local leaders, was 10 percent below the national figure of 4,860.

Having located the SCCs and developed a demographic profile of the six types based on our census returns, we embarked upon the main part of the study: learning about what motivated people to join SCCs, and what personal and social consequences they expected from membership. This information was obtained from the motivations survey. That survey was followed by the attitudes survey, designed to probe members, attitudes, beliefs, and behavior as Catholics, and to compare these findings with a national survey of Catholics.

The Motivations and Attitudes Surveys

The motivations and attitudes surveys (see Tables 4 and 5), carried out in the late winter and spring of 1996, were designed to be filled in by individual members of SCCs to reflect their personal reasons for joining SCCs, and their religious beliefs, attitudes, and actions. We again used random numbers to obtain groups (and alternates) to reflect the now known distributions of SCCs by type and subtype (the BV, the NAPRC, and so forth being subtypes of GSCs), and by diocese/region.

The contact persons for the groups that fell into the sample were telephoned and written to ensure their cooperation, and to inform us how many active members their groups included. We mailed covering letters, questionnaires, and return envelopes to match the number reported by the contact persons. Overall results appear in Tables 4 and 5.

Interviews and Observations

The final stage of data gathering took place in the period between February and June 1997. During February, we began making preparations for visits to each of the six SCC types to interview members and leaders, and to observe SCC gatherings. We hoped to carry out at least five interviews with members of each of the six SCC types, and to make at least five observations.

Appendix II / Table 4
Motivations Survey

SCC Type	Groups Sampled	Question-naires	Responses	Rate
	N	N	N	%
GSC	39	524	194	37%
H/L	16	346	86	25
Charismatics	12	227	67	30
CTA/ECC	14	402	208	52

Appendix II / Table 5
Attitudes Survey

SCC Type	Groups Sampled	Question-naires	Responses	Rate
	N	N	N	%
GSC	36	358	188	53%
H/L	11	500	36	7
Charismatics	7	249	105	42
CTA/ECC	21	423	217	51

To ready ourselves for the site visits, we held a weekend training session March 14–15, at Catholic University in Washington D.C. Two research assistants (Camille Corio and Bonnie Shreck) and R. R. Ekstrom of Loyola University, New Orleans, the project's grant administrator, attended. Two other participants in this phase of the research, Professors Patricia Killen and Jeanette Rodriguez (members of the theology team), who had prior experience with participant observation and interviewing, were unable to attend. However, training materials were mailed to them and discussed and reviewed with each by means of telephone conference calls. We also reviewed the instruments that had been developed for the interviews and observations.

The interview and observation instruments were an outgrowth of the December 1996 gathering of the research and theology teams, during which the objectives of the research were reviewed, and the goals for this phase determined. Follow-up refining of the instruments was done by telephone and FAX; they were pretested in late February and finalized after the March training session.

The major objective of the observations was to learn something about what people did when they gathered at regular group meetings. How long were the meetings? How formal or informal? Were there specific times devoted to prayer? To faith sharing? To scripture reading and discussion? To music? To quiet time? To other activities?

We recognized that the observations were going to be limited in nature—only one visit per group—thus providing only a snapshot in time. Still, we were hopeful that they would add some substance and human contact to the findings from our census and surveys.

The major objective of the interviews was to obtain a personal perspective on the experience of SCC membership. The dozen questions that formed the basis for the interviews included a brief review of the individual's spiritual/religious journey that led him or her to the group; the individual's perspective on group gatherings; how the SCC experience might have affected the individual's values and beliefs; and the individual's sense of the importance of being gathered and also of being sent, that is, of going forth to live the gospel.

There was a narrow time frame, from late March until the end of June, for the completion of the last stage of research. We were fortunate to have available two Spanish-speaking team members (Bonnie Schreck and Professor Jeanette Rodriguez) to interact with the Latinos. Five team members were available to interact with the other SCCs. Because of budgetary and time restrictions, we tried to arrange for at least two and if possible three interviews and two or more observations within each research site.

The sites were selected to reflect the diocesan regional distribution of SCCs. But it was also necessary to ascertain beforehand whether particular SCCs would be meeting during time periods we had available, and to ensure that we would be welcome. We used the telephone to assure ourselves of access and also to arrange interviews. In addition, the researchers were encouraged to find and add as many interviews as could be carried out within the span of their visits. Site visits lasted three, four, five, and occasionally six days, during which the researchers stayed at nearby motels.

We were able to complete a majority of our visits within six of the eight dioceses that had been the subject of our intensive census and survey activity. The remaining groups were located in dioceses within the same regions of the country. Overall, all eight diocesan regions were reflected in the members interviewed and the groups observed.

When the transcriptions were finished, we found that we had completed 40 interviews and 43 observations (Table 6).

Cancellations and calendar conflicts prevented us from completing interviews with SCC members from each type within each region. We had excellent cooperation from Latinos in Las Cruces and Fresno. We used Miami instead of Charlotte because we found that the SCC movement for Hispanics in Charlotte was in the embryonic stage; Miami has a movement that is full of life. Although the selections were based on accessibility and availability, we obtained rich data that have added much substance to the surveys.

The National Survey of Roman Catholics

We would know much more about small Christian communities in the U.S. Catholic Church if we knew not only critical information about SCCs and SCC members, but were able to compare and contrast them with Catholic life in the general U.S. Catholic population. For this reason, we secured the services of the Research Center of the University of Maryland to conduct a survey (by telephone) of the general Catholic population, asking for data on many of the same items for which we collected data from SCC communities and community members.

The survey questions were prepared in consultation with the research team and the team of theologians. They were pretested and critiqued in preparation of the instrument used in the survey.

Just over 800 interviews were conducted. In the data we used for comparison and contrast, we did not include those who identified themselves as having been born Catholic, but no longer consider themselves Catholic. That left us with a database of 667. We

Appendix II / Table 6
Distribution of Interviews and Observations

SCC Type	Interviews	Observations
GSC	6	9
H/L	11	9
CTA	8	3
ECC	7	10
Charismatics	4	6
Campus	4	6

asked these Catholics whether they belonged to a group with a religious or spiritual purpose. Approximately 40 percent said yes (266) and the remaining 60 percent (401) said no. In the tables in this book, Dr. Bernard Lee has compared SCC members with Catholics from the national survey who were not members of any kind of a religious group, since the 667 "All Catholics" would also include those who belonged to small Christian communities.

Summary

We used a wide range of sources to find, contact, and learn about the six types of small Christian communities that are the focus of this study. In this appendix we have described the various sampling procedures that enabled us to develop a broad national mapping of SCCs, and the sampling of dioceses by regions to enable our findings to be as representative of SCCs as possible. The census survey provided a demographic portrait of each of the SCC types; the motivations survey helped explain why individuals joined SCCs as well as the impact of such membership on their personal and parish lives; the attitudes survey enabled us to probe the attitudes, values, beliefs, and behavior of SCC members, and to compare them with a national representative sample of American Catholics. The interviews and observations enabled us to get some in-depth understanding of the impact of SCCs on individual members, and a glimpse of SCC gatherings. And, finally, the General Survey of U.S. Catholics provided a basis for comparing and contrasting SCC Catholics with the general Catholic population.

Note: those who might be interested in fuller technical data for professional reasons are invited to contact:

Dr. William V. D'Antonio
Dept. of Sociology/Life Cycle Institute
The Catholic University of America
620 Michigan Avenue, NE
Washington, DC 20064

Works Consulted

Banks, Robert. *Paul's Idea of Community: The Early House Churches in Their Historical Setting.* Grand Rapids: Eerdmans, 1980.

Baranowski, Arthur. *Creating Small Faith Communities: A Plan for Restructuring the Parish and Renewing Catholic Life.* Cincinnati: St. Anthony Messenger Press, 1988.

Bellah, Robert; Madsen, R.; Sullivan, W.; Swidler, A.; and Tipton, S. *Habits of the Heart: Individualism and Commitment in American Life.* Berkeley: University of California Press, 1985.

Branick, Vincent. *The House Church in the Writings of Paul.* Wilmington: Glazier, 1989.

Buber, Martin. *I and Thou.* New York: Charles Scribner's Sons, 1958.

Camille, Michael. *Image on the Edge: The Margins of Medieval Art.* Cambridge: Harvard University Press, 1992.

Cowan, Michael; Lee, B. *Conversation, Risk, and Conversion: The Inner and Public Life of Small Christian Communities.* Maryknoll: Orbis Books, 1997.

D'Antonio, William; Davidson, J.; Hoge, D.; and Wallace, R. *Laity American and Catholic: Transforming the Church.* Kansas City: Sheed & Ward, 1996.

Davidson, James; Williams, A.; Lamanna, R.; Stenftenagel, J.; Weigert, K.; Whalen, W.; and Wittberg, P. *The Search for Common Ground: What Unites and Divides Catholic Americans.* Huntington, Ind.: Our Sunday Visitor, 1997.

Dierks, Sheila D. *Women Eucharist*. Boulder, Colo.: Woven Word Press, 1997.

Dulles, Avery. *Models of the Church*. New York: Doubleday, 1974.

Dykstra, Craig. *Initiatives in Religion*. Indianapolis: Lilly Endowment, Inc., Winter 1998.

Farley, Edward. *Deep Symbols: Their Postmodern Effacement and Reclamation*. Valley Forge: Trinity International, 1997.

Geertz, Clifford. *After the Fact: Two Countries, Four Decades, One Anthropologist*. Cambridge: Harvard University Press, 1995.

Gutierrez, Gustavo. *The Truth Shall Make You Free*. Maryknoll: Orbis Books, 1990.

Hadaway, Kirk; Marler, P.; and Chaves, M. "What the Polls Don't Show: A Closer Look at U.S. Church Attendance." *American Sociological Review*, December, 1993, 58/6, 751–52.

Heschel, Abraham Joshua. *The Prophets*. Vol. 1. New York: Harper, 1962.

Jabes, Edmond. *The Book of Margins*. Chicago: University of Chicago Press, 1993.

James, William. *Varieties of Religious Experience*. New York: New American Library, 1958.

Kleissler, Thomas; LeBret, M.; and McGuinness, M. *Small Christian Communities: A Vision of Hope*. New York: Paulist Press, 1991.

Lee, Bernard. *The Future Church of 140 BCE: A Hidden Revolution*. New York: Crossroad, 1995.

Lee, Bernard; Cowan, M. *Dangerous Memories: House Churches and Our American Story*. Kansas City: Sheed & Ward, 1986.

Lohfink, Gerhard. *Jesus and Community*. Philadelphia: Fortress, 1984.

McBrien, Richard. *Catholicism*. San Francisco: Harper, 1994.

Meier, John. *A Marginal Jew: Rethinking the Historical Jesus*. Garden City: Doubleday, 1991.

The Official Catholic Directory Anno Domini 1993. P. J. Kenedy & Sons, with R. R. Bowker. New Providence, N.J.: Reed Reference Publishing, 1994.

Overman, J. Andrew. *Church and Community in Crisis: The Gospel According to Matthew.* Valley Forge: Trinity International, 1996.

Rahner, Karl. *The Shape of the Church to Come.* New York: Seabury, 1974.

Riesman, David; Glazer, N.; and Denney, R. *The Lonely Crowd: A Study of the Changing American Character.* New Haven: Yale University Press, 1961.

Sennett, Richard. *The Fall of Public Man.* New York: Vintage Books, 1978.

Slater, Philip. *The Pursuit of Loneliness: American Culture at the Breaking Point.* Boston: Beacon, 1970.

de Tocqueville, Alexis. *Democracy in America.* Garden City: Doubleday, 1969.

Turner, Victor. *The Ritual Process: Structure and Anti-Structure.* New York: Cornell University Press, 1969.

Vandenakker, John. *Small Christian Communities and the Parish.* Kansas City: Sheed & Ward, 1994.

Veling, Terry. *Living in the Margins: Intentional Communities and the Art of Interpretation.* New York: Crossroad, 1996.

Whitehead, Evelyn Eaton; Whitehead, J. D. *Community of Faith: Crafting Christian Communities Today.* Mystic, Conn.: Twenty-Third Publications, 1992.

Wittberg, Patricia. *Pathways to Re-Creating Religious Communities.* New York: Paulist Press, 1996.

Wuthnow, Robert. *Sharing the Journey: Support Groups and America's New Quest for Community.* New York: Macmillan Free Press, 1994.